Eco-nomics

Eco-nomics

WHAT EVERYONE SHOULD KNOW ABOUT ECONOMICS AND THE ENVIRONMENT

Richard L. Stroup

CATO
INSTITUTE
Washington, D.C.

Library of Congress Cataloging-in-Publication Data

Stroup, Richard.
    Eco-nomics : what everyone should know about economics and the
environment / Richard L. Stroup.
        p. cm.
    Includes bibliographical references and index.
    ISBN 1-930865-44-9 (pbk. : alk. paper)
        1. Environmental economics. 2. Environmental policy--Economic
aspects. I. Title.

HC79.E5S775 2003
333.7--dc21   2003043783

Cover design by Elise Rivera.
Cover photography © Comstock Images.
Printed in the United States of America.

CATO INSTITUTE
1000 Massachusetts Ave., N.W.
Washington, D.C. 20001
www.cato.org

Contents

Introduction

The Forest Guardians, an advocacy group based in Santa Fe, New Mexico, sued the federal government to stop logging on the national forests in New Mexico. The group thought that the forests should be preserved rather than cut down, and it pushed for such policies during the 1990s.

In 2000 a fire began around Los Alamos, New Mexico, that eventually wiped out many of the forests that the Guardians wanted to preserve. When the fire was over, Rex Wahl, executive director of the Forest Guardians, reconsidered his position. "Judicious cutting of small tress is what's needed," he said.

This example illustrates one of the problems with environmental issues. Things are not always what they seem. The Forest Guardians thought that its goal should be to preserve trees. Yet by ignoring the need to thin the forest and remove dead and dying trees, they allowed the forest to become vulnerable to wildfire, and the ultimate destruction of the forests was much greater.

It's one thing to be passionate about protecting the environment. It's another thing to be successful at it. Many laws have been enacted in the United States to clean up pollution or preserve natural beauty, but many of them have unintended consequences. They don't save the species they were supposed to. Or they don't clean up the rivers as Congress intended. They end up costing a lot of money, often creating large government bureaucracies that can't seem to achieve the goals that seemed within reach when the agency was formed or the law was passed.

On the positive side, the air and the water in North America are getting cleaner, and a lot of land retains its natural qualities. Indeed, lakes and rivers that were dirty have been cleaned, and more and more Americans are able to live in surroundings that they find pleasant.

This book helps explain the paradox—why many of our laws don't work but why, at the same time, countries like the United

States and Canada are becoming more attractive by maintaining or restoring their natural beauty. This is a short book, only four chapters long, and it cannot cover every reason that explains the paradox. Nor will it present all of the options for moving forward or offer all of the reasons why it is hard-going.

Yet for those who can be dispassionate—that is, objective and analytical about environmental issues—it is a useful guide. This book can make sense of a lot that is happening around us. Perhaps you might think about taking it with you as you head out to the beach or to the mountains. It might help you explain over the campfire how the streams can be kept clean and the woods pristine. And it may encourage you to think more about these problems when you return home.

1. Scarcity: An Economics Primer

This chapter introduces 10 principles of economics that shed light on environmental problems. They are presented as the answers to commonly asked questions about environmental issues. It should quickly become clear that economics is about choice, not necessarily about money, and that economics can help us understand environmental choices, both public and private.

1. In a land as rich as the United States, why do we face so many difficult choices about the environment?

Scarcity, even in a nation as wealthy as the United States, is always with us, so choices must be made.

We have vast forests in this country but not enough to provide all of the wood, all of the wilderness, and all of the accessible recreation that we want. As soon as we log trees, build roads, or improve trails and campsites, we lose some wilderness. Similarly, we have large amounts of fresh water, but if we use water to grow rice in California, the water consumed cannot be used for drinking water in California cities. If we use fire to help a forest renew itself, we will have air pollution downwind while the fire burns. We have many goals, so we have to make choices about how to allocate our limited resources. The cost of those choices is what we give up— the cost of opportunities lost.

Trouble is, people have differing goals and disagree about which choice is the best one. Pursuit of differing goals may lead to conflict. Nowhere is this clearer than in environmental matters.

California's San Bernardino County was about to build a new hospital. Less than 24 hours before groundbreaking, the U.S. Fish and Wildlife Service announced that the flower-loving Delhi Sands fly, which had been found on the site, was an endangered species. So the county had to spend $4.5 million to move the hospital 250 feet to give the flies a few acres to live on and a corridor to the

1

nearby sand dunes. It also had to divert funds from its medical mission to pay for biological studies of the fly.[1]

Environmentalists who want biological diversity were relieved that the hospital would move, but county officials were upset at the delay and the high cost that its hospital budget and the taxpayers would have to bear. To use resources one way sacrifices the use of those resources for other things. There is no escaping cost.

San Bernardino County faced a choice between timely provision of a health care facility and protection of a unique species. Often the choices, however, are between different environmental goals. Our old-growth forests can be preserved, but that means giving up the enhanced recreation and wildlife appreciation that trails and campsites bring for many people. Strict preservation (which is what a wilderness designation means) also means that trees can't be thinned to minimize insect infestations and potentially catastrophic fires. In that case, the choice could be between keeping old-growth trees standing—until the next fire—or cutting some of them down so that more of them will be saved in the long run.

Scarcity is a fundamental fact of life, not just of economics. It is always present in nature, even when human beings are not. Each population of a species can flourish and expand only until it reaches the limit of available habitat, sunlight, water, and nutrients. Trees grow taller as they compete for sunlight. Some plants spread their leaves horizontally, capturing sunlight while blocking access for other species that might sprout up to compete for water and nutrients. Each successful strategy captures resources, taking them from certain competing species populations.

Competition implies that some species will lose out. This loss can happen slowly over time as change occurs. When a niche in the habitat changes, each population, using a different strategy, gains or loses relative to its competitors. Even small changes in a habitat can change the competitive outcome and reallocate space, water, and nutrients among populations of various species. Every change in a local environment will favor some species at the expense of others. And local environments are always changing over time, whether humans are present or not.

---

[1] William Booth, "Flower-Loving Insect Becomes Symbol for Opponents of Endangered Species Act," *Washington Post*, April 4, 1997, A-1.

In other words, scarcity and competition are not ideas that are limited to selfish human beings.

2. Even though economists emphasize selfish motives, don't people have common goals? Doesn't everyone want a safe and attractive environment?

People share many values, but each person has a narrow focus and somewhat different purposes; each person wants to emphasize different goals.

The goals of some individuals are selfish—intended to further only their own welfare. The goals of others are altruistic—intended to help their fellowman. In both cases, each person's concerns and vision are focused mainly on a narrow set of ends.

Even the most noble and altruistic goals are typically narrow. Consider a couple of famous examples. The concern felt by the late Mother Teresa for the indigent and the sick of Calcutta was legendary. So, too, was Sierra Club founder John Muir's love of wilderness and his focus on protecting wilderness for all time. In both cases their goals were widely regarded as noble and altruistic, not narrowly selfish.

Yet one might be tempted to consider that Mother Teresa would have been willing to sacrifice some of the remaining wilderness in India in order to provide another hospital for the people she cared so much about—those dying in Calcutta. And John Muir would have been willing to see fewer hospitals if that helped preserve wilderness. Individuals with unselfish goals, like all others, are narrowly focused. Each individual is willing to see sacrifices made in other less important goals in order to further his or her own narrow purposes.

As Adam Smith, the founder of classical economics, pointed out more than 200 years ago, we know and care most about things that directly affect us, our immediate family, and others close to us. We know much less about things that mostly affect people we never see. When a person furthers his or her narrow set of goals, it doesn't mean that the individual cares nothing about others. It just means that for each of us, our strongest interests are narrowly focused. These narrow sets of goals, whatever the mix of selfishness and altruism, correspond to what economists call the "self-interest" of that individual.

It is unavoidable that an individual's choices will be driven by a narrow focus. Thus, people who call themselves environmentalists may differ from others who place a higher priority on providing good schools or hospitals or making sure that poor people are well provided for. And they may also differ on which environmental goals to pursue. There are thousands of worthy environmental goals, but each competes with others for our limited land, water, and other resources. Even without selfishness, the narrow focus of individuals is enough to ensure that there will be strong disagreements and competition for scarce natural resources.

This narrowness of emphasis is important for understanding the economics of environmental issues. Depending on the circumstances, narrow goals can lead to tunnel vision, with destructive results, or to satisfying exchanges that make all participants better-off.

3. Why do fierce arguments between organizations and individuals erupt over decisions about our resources and environment?

Although scarcity guarantees competition, some forms of competition lead to constructive action that reduces scarcity, while other forms are destructive.

Disagreement on values is normal. Some environmentalists who strongly appreciate the recreational and aesthetic benefits of wild, free-flowing rivers propose that dams be removed around the nation. Other people who value the flood protection, recreation, and clean hydropower provided by the dams want to preserve them. Similarly, wilderness advocates lobby to prevent the construction of new roads in roadless areas, while people who want greater public access to the same lands lobby for additional roads and campgrounds.

The same lands and rivers cannot simultaneously provide the advantages of preservation in a wild state and the benefits of development to improve access and the delivery of other services. Competition over the management of these rivers and lands is inevitable. The only question is the form that competition will take.

Human competition can be violent or it can be peaceful and constructive. Markets are generally peaceful. Even the repellent term "cutthroat competition" refers to a constructive activity: It means offering buyers low prices in order to get them to buy something. Sellers compete for buyers by improving their products and lowering their costs.

4

Human competition can also be destructive. Wars are the prime example, of course, but competition can be destructive even when it is not violent. Political battles, for example, can result in costly and unpleasant smear campaigns by various sides, each seeking to take votes from the other.

4. As people seek to meet their goals, can we predict how they will choose among the many ways they can advance those goals?

Yes.

Incentives matter.

Nearly everyone would want to save a person who is drowning. But each of us is more likely to try to rescue a person who falls into two feet of water at the edge of a small pond than to try to rescue someone who falls over the edge of Niagara Falls. In other words, whatever the goal, we can predict that people will more likely act to achieve it when the cost to them is minimal, and will seek low-cost ways—low cost to themselves and their goals—to do so. These costs and benefits—or penalties and rewards—are called incentives.

Incentives help us to understand behavior. If a person's goal is to increase his or her income, that person has an incentive to devote long hours to a grueling job. If federal taxpayers can help pay the cost of a highway in one state, the state legislature has an additional incentive to build the highway. If people can protect an endangered species without disrupting their lives, they are more likely to choose to save it.

Incentives also affect the methods people use to achieve a particular goal. For example, to generate electricity from burning coal requires water for cooling. But how much water? Evaporative cooling consumes more water than coolers that work like a car radiator, recirculating the water. But using more water by evaporating it can get more electricity from the same coal. Where water is more expensive, generating companies will probably choose to use more coal and less water by using recirculating cooling methods. But where water is cheaper, generators will use more water, evaporating it into air, and save on coal. Operating steam-electric power plants can use as little as 1.3 gallons of water to generate a kilowatt-hour of electricity, or as much as 170 gallons, depending on the relative cost of water.

It is not difficult for us as individuals to recognize and evaluate the cost of different choices. We are well-tuned to the relative costs to us of alternatives that are available to us. However, it's more difficult to recognize and take into account the costs facing others. Costs to others will have less effect on our choices than the costs—and benefits—that we incur directly.

Typically, we expect people in business or individuals seeking personal goals to be more sensitive to their own costs than to those of others. We sometimes assume that government officials will not be. But a well-known court case brought by South Carolina developer David Lucas shows that officials of South Carolina were also more sensitive to their own costs than to those of their constituents.[2]

The saga began when the state passed a law regulating construction along its coastline, presumably to preserve open space and to prevent possible erosion. David Lucas owned two lots along the shore, but once the law was passed, officials told him that he could not build there, even though people next to his property had already built homes on their shoreline properties.

Lucas lost nearly all the value of his land. He believed that if the state wanted to control his land for a public purpose (other than stopping him from harming other people or property), the state should pay for it. So he sued to force payment. Initially, Lucas lost, but he appealed all the way to the U.S. Supreme Court and finally won. The court told South Carolina that it must pay for the land because it had taken from Lucas the same rights to use it that his neighbors enjoyed.

Once the state was faced with having to pay Lucas more than $1 million, officials changed their minds about keeping the land from development. In fact, the state sold the land to a developer!

Earlier, when they thought Lucas would pay the cost of stopping development, state regulators had little incentive to worry about the cost. But when forced to bear the cost from their own budget, they made the opposite decision: They allowed development. Incentives mattered.

The Endangered Species Act illustrates the harm that can occur when one party (in this case, the government) determines how another (in this case, landowners) must use land. Under the act,

[2]More details about the Lucas case can be found in James R. Rinehart and Jeffrey J. Pompe, "The Lucas Case and the Conflict over Property Rights," in *Land Rights: The 1990s' Property Rights Rebellion,* Bruce Yandle, ed. (Lanham, Md.: Rowman & Littlefield, 1995), 67–101.

government officials have great latitude in telling landowners what to do if they find an endangered animal such as a red-cockaded woodpecker on their properties. The government chooses the protection methods, but the landowner must pay the costs. For example, the owner may not be allowed to log land within a certain distance of the bird's colony. In some cases, government officials have prevented discing (that is, plowing up land to create a firebreak) and even farming. With this power, the government is likely to be lavishly wasteful of some resources (such as land) while ignoring other ways of protecting the species (such as building nest boxes). To the government agency, the land is almost a free good.

The point of these two examples is that when people have to pay for what they use, they carefully weigh the costs and benefits.

Although incentives are important, they are not the only factors in decisionmaking. For example, income levels affect how people deal with environmental problems. People with high incomes tend to have more concern about the protection of natural environments, such as old-growth timber or the habitat for rare plants or animals. Those with lower incomes frequently want to see those same lands managed to produce more food, raw materials, and jobs. Very poor people, wanting the basics of environmental protection such as drinking water free of parasites and microbial diseases in order to stay alive, may not be able to go much beyond that to effect environmental quality, even if given some incentive to do so. The same incentive may not have the same effect on people in different circumstances.

Other factors matter, too. Cultural norms and traditions affect how people value various parts of their environment. Whether people toss litter on the ground or out of a car window reflects their education and probably the attitudes of those with whom they associate.

5. In market exchange, people can only gain at the expense of others— right?

Wrong!

Voluntary exchange—that is, market trading—*creates* wealth.

It's amazing but true that simple voluntary exchange can create wealth. Both sides can gain. One way to understand this principle is to think about something that people really disagree about—say, music. John likes opera. Jane likes rock music. If John has a rock concert ticket, and Jane an opera ticket, just exchanging the tickets will make each person wealthier.

Trade can create value in three ways:

1. Trade channels resources, products, and services from those who value them less to those who value them more. Without any change in production, the trade of the opera ticket for the rock concert ticket produces value.
2. Trade enables individuals to direct their resources to the activities where they produce the greatest value so that they can then trade the fruits of those activities for the items they want for themselves. The farmer in central Montana who grows wheat produces far more than he wants to consume. He trades the wheat for income to buy coffee from Guatemala, shoes from Thailand, and oranges from Florida. The Montana farmer might have been able to grow oranges, but given the cold Montana climate, doing so would have squandered resources. Trade enables people to obtain many things they would not have the proper talent or resources to produce efficiently themselves.
3. Trade enables everyone to gain from the division of labor and from economies of scale. Only with trade can individuals specialize narrowly in computer programming, writing books, or playing professional golf—developing highly productive skills that would be impossible to obtain if each family had to produce everything for itself. Similarly, the sales of large automobile factories that bring the cost of cars within reach of the average worker would not be feasible without large-scale trade that enables the product of one factory to be sold in a wide market area.

Resource owners gain by trading in three different ways: across uses (for example, out of low-valued crops into ones that earn more money), across space (marketing products across geographic distance to different states or nations), and across time (gaining from conservation or speculation by saving resources until they become more valuable).

Many farmers in the western United States own rights to divert and use water from streams to produce crops. In recent years, more people have been seeking high-quality streams for fly-fishing. They recognize that many streams have a tendency to dry up in hot summer months when farmers divert large amounts of water for their fields. These fly-fishers may want more water kept in streams to keep fish thriving. To keep the streams full of water, some fishers are willing to trade cash for the farmers' water rights. And some farmers are happy to part with a portion of the water they have been using in exchange for cash.

That exchange is being done in Oregon. Andrew Purkey of the Oregon Water Trust works out trades between his organization, which is committed to protecting salmon, and farmers who are willing to give up some of their water. For example, Purkey paid a rancher $6,000 to not grow hay one year. The water the rancher would have used stayed in the stream and supported the fish.

Other farmers might gain by selling some of their water rights to growing cities, which can then save the cost (and the environmental disturbance) of building another dam—or a saltwater desalinization plant to make fresh water from ocean water. When such trades among willing buyers and willing sellers are allowed by law, both buyer and seller are made better-off. Value is added to the water's use. Wealth is created. Unfortunately, right now the federal government and many Western states have laws that pose obstacles to trade in water. These obstacles, such as the rule that only some uses of water are allowed, tend to keep the water in agriculture, reducing efficient use and conservation.

Even trade in garbage can create wealth. Consider a city that disposes of garbage in a landfill. If the city is located in an area where underground water lies near the surface, disposing of garbage is dangerous, and very costly measures would have to be taken to protect the water from leakage. Such a city may gain by finding a trading partner with more suitable land where a properly constructed landfill does not threaten to pollute water. Such a landowner may be willing to accept garbage in return for pay. If so, both parties will be better-off.

6. What do profits achieve for the environment? And for that matter, what do they do for consumers?

In a competitive market, profits and losses direct businesses toward activities that increase consumer wealth and conserve resources.

Profits attract producers and sellers. Where there is profit to be made, consumers benefit from the increased competition to produce the good or service. And profits lead to careful use of natural resources because, to make profits, producers must minimize their costs.

Producers spend untold hours figuring out how to save on resources in search of increased profit. That's why soda cans weigh at least 27 percent less than they did in the 1960s, why steel high-rise buildings today require about one-third the amount of steel they needed several decades ago, and why a fiber-optic cable made from 60 pounds of sand can carry 1,000 times more information than a cable made from 2,000 pounds of copper.[3]

Profits reward those who succeed in producing goods and services that people are willing to buy at a price higher than the cost of supplying them. Losses have their place, too. They penalize those who have not been able to discover how to create more value than the cost to produce. In effect, people are telling a money-losing firm that they want to see the firm's resources go to other products or services that are more valuable to them.

Large profits have a way of disappearing. The competition of new entrants, drawn by profits, gradually lowers the sales of existing firms and often their prices as well, reducing the level of those profits. Entry continues until profits fall to what economists call normal rates of return. Entry then stops. The first firms to innovate successfully may make above-normal profits, but the profit rate falls as competition heats up.

Usually, an entrepreneur seeking to exploit a new profit opportunity must (a) discover the new opportunity, and (b) find investors willing to take the risk that profits will in fact be gained. It may also be necessary to sell potential buyers on the new product or service. All of these activities are costly. But expected profit provides an incentive to persevere for entrepreneurs, investors, and those who must sell the idea to investors and the product to buyers. It rewards them for making the necessary investments of time, effort, and money to accomplish their tasks. New ideas may need years of effort before they reach fruition. Expected profit is the carrot to attract the needed efforts.

[3]Lynn Scarlett, *New Environmentalism*, NCPA Policy Report 201 (Dallas: National Center for Policy Analysis, January 1997), 11.

Which producers win the competition for the use of scarce resources? Investors and producers who expect more profit are willing to pay more when necessary to get resources for successful production. Those who expect losses are not willing (and those already experiencing losses are less able) to compete for those same resources. Taking resources from high-valued to low-valued uses in a market setting imposes losses on those who do so. Moving resources to higher-valued uses confers profits. Losses discipline investors and producers whose expectations were too optimistic, while profits reward those who make the best use, as seen by consumers, of the available resources.

7. Information is the resource of the modern age; every decision should be made with full information. Right?
Wrong again!

Information is a valuable, but costly, resource.

Let's say that a private owner decides to build a landfill for garbage. The owner is liable for damages if waste deposited in the landfill leaks out and harms others. So the owner must decide how to prevent leaks and how to clean them up if they occur. Spending too little on preventing harm from escaping pollutants could bring costly lawsuits. But spending more than is necessary imposes needless costs and wastes resources. How many resources should be devoted to preventing harm? In other words, how much should be spent? That is the question facing the owner.

To make the decision, good information is crucial. Yet gathering more information (Where is the groundwater underneath this land? How effective will a clay cap be? What liner will be the safest?) to make a better decision also is costly.

This owner, operating in the private sector, has an incentive to gather just enough information—not too much and not too little— because both the costs and the benefits of seeking more information fall upon the owner. Weighing the costs and benefits of more information, the owner won't end up with perfect or complete information but will make a reasonable choice based on the costs and benefits of seeking more knowledge.

Now suppose that a government regulator (perhaps someone in the local zoning office) has the authority to decide whether the landfill can be built. This individual's desire for information will be much different. If damage occurs, the regulator could be blamed, so his or her incentive will be to require as much information possible before allowing the landfill to be built. Further, the regulator doesn't face the costs of seeking more information or the costs of choosing the most expensive way to reduce risks from the landfill. The regulator may ask for study after study to make sure that the proposed landfill will really be safe. Not surprisingly, people running small businesses often complain that regulators are simply asking for too much paperwork.

In other words, the information-gathering process is affected by where the costs fall. A regulator might demand too much information, but under some conditions the owner might seek too little. Suppose the property rights of neighbors are not effectively protected under law, and the private owner of the waste site is not accountable for harm caused by materials escaping the site. In that case, the owner may minimize the cost of preventing pollutants from seeping out of the site, trusting that the costs of any harm will fall on others. The incentive to seek additional information is weak because the owner doesn't expect to pay the costs of making a poor decision.

Important decisions require good information. Should a forest be cut now and replanted? Should the owner of a potentially polluting hazardous waste site be forced to spend several million dollars in a cleanup effort? Should mineral exploration for new mineral deposits be conducted now or later? Should an environmental rule be further tightened?

Each of these decisions involves gathering scarce and costly information, and each decision must be made without complete information. But the information-gathering process will be shaped by the incentives facing the decisionmaker.

8. New technology may be cheaper, but doesn't it destroy the environment? Wouldn't we be better-off, environmentally, if only older, tried-and-true technologies are allowed?
No.

Advanced technologies typically help the environment because they decrease resource waste and increase resource productivity.

Sometimes we wish for the good old days before we suffered from the pollution and congestion caused by automobiles. But our ancestors didn't think of cars that way. To them, the advent of the automobile was a blessing since it meant that horses no longer clogged the streets with horse manure. And today, thousands, perhaps millions, of acres have reverted to forest because the land is no longer devoted to growing grass and hay for horses. Also, new farming technologies allow for more production from fewer acres, freeing still more land for reversion to habitat and recreation.

Yes, the automobile does pollute. But today's cars emit a tiny fraction of the pollution emitted by the cars of the early 1970s. And while even very expensive and clean-running electric cars require energy from burning fuel in power plants, the emissions from such plants have gone down drastically, too, as owners have searched out low-sulfur coal and technical devices to reduce pollution. Advances in technology continue to make cars cleaner and safer, just as diesel train engines replaced dirty steam locomotives, and gas and electricity replaced coal for home heating.

New technology is almost always adopted because it is more efficient. It usually uses fewer resources to produce the same result. Stifling new technology unnecessarily forces us to forgo additional gains that could be delivered over time.

9. If the rich countries would just stop consuming so much, couldn't we all live more comfortably on this planet?
No.

As people's incomes increase, their willingness to pay for protecting the environment increases.

Even poor communities are willing to make sacrifices for some basic components of environmental protection, such as access to safe and clean drinking water and sanitary handling of human and animal wastes. As incomes rise, citizens raise their environmental goals. Once basic demands for food, clothing, and shelter are met, people demand cleaner air, cleaner streams, more outdoor recreation, and the protection of wild lands. With higher incomes, citizens place higher priorities on environmental objectives.

The connection of income with better environmental quality has been noted numerous times by economists. One study, for example, showed that in countries where rising incomes reached about $6,000 to $8,000 per year in 2001 dollars and where there initially was an increase in certain types of air pollution, air pollution began to decline.[4] Also, the kinds of water and air pollution (indoor air pollution and water with parasites or micro-organisms) that very poor people confront fell steadily with rising incomes.

Another study suggests that the willingness of citizens to spend and sacrifice for a better environment rises far faster than income itself increases—more than twice as fast, according to recent economic research.[5] (That same willingness and ability to pay for a better environment falls with falling income.) The fact that readers of *Sierra* magazine (most of whom are members of the Sierra Club) have incomes almost twice as high as that of average Americans is another indicator that there is a link between income and active concern about environmental matters.

One implication of this link is that the wealthier the people of North America, the more concerned about the environment they will be. Similarly, if incomes fall, people will be less interested in environmental protection. Policymakers should also recognize that if improvement in environmental quality can be achieved at a lower cost—rather than wasted through bureaucratic red tape, for example—public support for additional environmental measures will be greater. Policies that do not deliver good environmental quality at the least cost to the economy needlessly reduce the citizens' willingness and ability to pay for environmental quality measures.

10. What is the single most common error in thinking about the economics of environmental policy?

The most common error in economics, as in ecology, is to ignore the secondary effects and long-term consequences of an action.

It is easy to overlook the unintended side effects of an action, especially if those effects will not be experienced soon. When individuals are not personally accountable for the full costs of their actions, they tend to ignore the secondary costs of what they do.

Consider the classic case of overgrazing on a commons, a pasture open to all herdsmen for cattle grazing. Each herdsman captures the immediate benefits of grazing another cow, but may hardly be aware of the reduction in next year's grass that the extra animal

[4]Gene M. Grossman and Alan B. Krueger, "Economic Growth and the Environment," *Quarterly Journal of Economics* 110, no. 2 (1995), 353–77.

[5]Don Coursey, *The Demand for Environmental Quality*. (St. Louis, Mo.: John M. Olin School of Business, Washington University, December 1992).

grazing this year is causing. The individual herdsman is forced to bear only a fraction of the costs—the reduced grazing available next year due to excessive grazing now—because all users share the future costs. If the herdsman removed his cow, he would bear fully the burden of reducing his use. Thus, each herdsman has an incentive to add cows, even though the pasture may be gradually deteriorating as a result. This situation is known as the tragedy of the commons.

A similar problem can occur when a fishing territory is open to all fishers. Each fisher captures all the benefits of harvesting more fish now, while paying only a small part of the future costs—the reduction of the fish population for future harvest. It is easy to ignore the indirect costs that will occur in the future, especially if the fisher will not ultimately pay the full, true cost of his or her actions.

Government decisionmaking provides additional examples. It is typical for cities to be years behind in the maintenance of their water delivery systems. The cost of a repair that will reduce water leaks is borne now, while much of the benefit lies in the future. The present costs tend to be more vividly seen and felt than the future benefits, so repairs are often postponed, even though that makes the future costs much larger. Because the costs of postponement are not as direct and are not immediate tend to encourage the costly postponement of maintenance.

Conclusion

These 10 points provide a good start toward understanding how economics applies to environmental decisionmaking. These principles lay the foundation for understanding, first, how cooperation can help to protect the environment and, second, why conflict often occurs instead. Cooperation is the subject of Chapter 2.

2. Rights: How Property Rights and Markets Replace Conflict with Cooperation

Tom Bourland faced a challenge. As a wildlife biologist at International Paper Company, one of the world's largest private forest owners, he wanted the forests to teem with wildlife like deer, bears, beaver, and woodpeckers. He didn't want his company simply to produce wood and pulp. Experimental efforts by the company proved that it was possible to enrich the forests in Louisiana and east Texas with wildlife, but doing so was costly. How could he make the improvement of wildlife habitat an integral part of the company's goals?

Bourland found a way. He knew that hunters, fishers, and campers love the woods as well as he does and would pay for the opportunity to use it, but only if the woods were full of wildlife, and diverse vegetation. So he began a program to market the recreational opportunities of that land. Once he began to make some money for International Paper this way, he had the clout needed to enhance the habitat. He could expand his use of prescribed burns to encourage new vegetation, for example, and he could prohibit logging next to streams to keep the water clean so fish would thrive.[1]

Many people think of protecting the environment as a struggle characterized by noisy, bitter, and protracted political conflicts. In the Pacific Northwest, for example, communities have been divided for many years as loggers and conservationists square off over how much land should be logged and how much should be set aside for the northern spotted owl and other endangered species. Yet Bourland's experience indicates that preservation does not have to be a struggle.

[1]For more about Bourland's project, see Terry L. Anderson and Donald R. Leal, *Enviro-Capitalists: Doing Good While Doing Well* (Lanham, Md.: Rowman & Littlefield, 1997), 4–8.

Competition and conflict are inevitable in a world of scarcity, and they will occur whether markets or the government are the vehicles to achieve environmental protection. However, a market society can channel energy and enthusiasm into constructive action that often achieves both protection of the land and use of its resources, as is done in the southeastern forests owned by International Paper.

Markets minimize political conflict because they depend on voluntary cooperation. Competitors increase their market power and wealth by providing what consumers want at low cost. When ownership is clear and wrongful harm is forbidden, competitors cannot use force to increase their power, but must cooperate with others for mutual gain.

But sometimes the ingredients necessary for the smooth channeling of competition into productive activities are missing. This chapter shows how privately held property rights and market exchange encourage cooperation and conservation, and also shows what happens when the necessary ingredients are missing.

1. Property rights are a necessary condition for market exchange.

A market is a place where property rights are traded. A property right is the right to use something, the right to exclude others from using it, and usually the right to sell, rent, or lease it. The person who purchases a farm, for example, is buying the owner's right to the exclusive use of that farm, the right to rent or lease the land to others, and the right to sell it later.

For a market to function properly, property rights must satisfy three conditions. They must be defined, defendable, and divestible, or "three-D." Markets can be effective only to the degree that property rights are three-D.

Rights must be defined. Most goods and services that we deal with every day are well-defined. In fact, a lot of effort goes into making sure exactly what they include. Before purchase, land is often surveyed and the boundaries of property are recorded in a local government office so that any dispute about where one person's property ends and another's begins can be easily settled. The rights that go with owning land vary. How much noise is allowed there? Is burning wood in a fireplace permitted? A potential buyer would be unwilling to spend much money on a new home if ownership and ownership rights were not clearly defined.

Sometimes, however, ownership isn't defined at all. The water flowing in most streams in the eastern United States has no owner, although the owners of property next to the water have a right to reasonable use of that water. No one really owns wildlife, either, although state governments have some level of control over it.

And sometimes ownership, while defined in theory, is not clearly defined in practice. People may be unsure about the precise boundaries of their properties. A fence on the boundary of two pieces of property might be poorly maintained if neither landowner is sure who owns it. Uncertainty about the definition of property rights and who is responsible for the property's upkeep reduces its value.

In recent years, environmental regulations have made the definition of land ownership unclear. For example, regulatory bodies such as the California Coastal Commission have required some landholders to provide public access to their lands. Some regulatory bodies have forbidden building homes on certain property (even when no harm to the property of others can be proved). Under the Endangered Species Act, the federal government can limit the way that land is used to protect habitat. Such situations make the effective ownership unclear, especially to owners of property that is nearby or in similar situations. Uncertainty about ownership lowers the value of property.

If the rights to a resource or a good are not defined or are poorly defined, the value of that resource falls. Potential buyers will be unwilling to pay much for the ownership of rights that aren't clear.

Rights must be defendable. Usually in the United States, property rights are readily defended. The courts will back an owner's property rights. However, if for any reason rights to a resource are difficult to defend against theft, harm, or trespass, the value of the resource falls.

A farmer's land that is too easily accessible to others can be robbed of its produce. The smell from a newly established hog-feeding operation may invade an owner's property. The land may become contaminated by hazardous waste from an unknown source. If the owner is unable to fully defend his or her ownership rights, the property is worth less than it would be otherwise.

The government can take away some elements of property rights through excessive regulation. For example, when the government designates land as a wetland, the U.S. Army Corps of Engineers can demand that landowners either not disturb it or pay the costs of adding wetlands elsewhere.

Regulations to stop actions that would harm others (causing a flood, for example) are a legitimate use of the government's police power. However, regulations that instead require a person to provide a public service (such as protecting a wetland without payment) may violate his or her property rights. The courts have been addressing these issues in recent years and have restricted the government's ability to make such regulatory demands without compensation.

Rights must be divestible. If property rights to a resource are not *divestible*, meaning that the owner is not free to sell or lease the resource at will, the resource is not likely to be well used.

In normal day-to-day living, we can usually sell what we own. The classified sections of most newspapers are filled with advertisements for property being offered by its owners—everything from used furniture to automobiles and boats. Most people take for granted the ability to buy and sell property. But there are important exceptions to some owners' ability to divest their land or resources.

In the recent past, it was common for people to save on inheritance taxes by providing property to a son or daughter, but holding it in trust for the grandchildren. The son or daughter could only obtain the income from it, not the full value of selling the property. This tended to distort decisions about how to use and care for the property. The middle generation had an incentive to increase its income by overusing the land, thus decreasing its long-term value.

On most American Indian reservations, federal laws have led to a situation where, when ownership of certain land is passed from one generation to another, it must be divided among an increasing number of heirs. Reaching agreement among the heirs on what to do with the property becomes difficult, thus limiting the ability of the owners to transfer the property.

The ability to divest property has enormous—but often unrecognized—effects, as a *Wall Street Journal* cartoon illustrates: A husband and wife are walking out of a home. The man says to the woman, "Their house looks so nice. They must be getting ready to sell it." The motivation to obtain maximum value from a potential buyer encourages people to maintain and improve their property.

20

"Their house looks so nice. They must be getting ready to sell it."

2. Private ownership and protection of property rights provide each resource owner with both the means and the incentive to protect and conserve the resource.

Very simply, property rights hold people accountable. When people treat property negligently or carelessly, its value decreases. When they treat it with care, its value increases. Aristotle recognized this point more than 2,000 years ago when he said, "What is common to many is taken least care of, for all men have greater regard for what is their own than for what they possess in common with others."[2]

Property rights must be protected by law. In a society that protects property rights, their resources, including themselves, from harm. Such harms include not only theft and assault but also pollution.

This protection occurs through the courts. In the United States, Canada, and other nations having legal roots in Great Britain, the courts have for centuries provided a way to stop individuals from injuring others by polluting. When a pollution victim shows that harm has been done or that serious harm is threatened, courts can force compensation or issue an injunction to stop the polluting activity. Such court suits are sometimes called private law but, more

---

[2] Aristotle, as quoted by Will Durant in *The Life of Greece* (New York: Simon and Schuster, 1939), 536.

generally, common law. Common law refers to the body of legal rules and traditions that have been developed over time through court decisions. Each decision helps to settle the details of the law, putting everyone on notice of what is expected, reducing uncertainty and thus the need for future legal action.

It is easy to find examples of common law protection against pollution, even going back more than 100 years. In the late 19th century, the Carmichael family owned a 45-acre farm in Texas, with a stream running through it, that bordered on the state of Arkansas.[3] The city of Texarkana, Arkansas, built a sewage system that deposited sewage in the river in front of the Carmichaels' home. They sued the city in federal court on the grounds that their family and livestock no longer were able to use the river and possibly were exposed to disease.

The court awarded damages to the Carmichaels and granted an injunction against the city, forcing it to stop the harmful dumping. Even though the city of Texarkana was operating properly under state law in building a sewer system, it could not foul the water used by the Carmichaels. Indeed, the judge noted, "I have failed to find a single well-considered case where the American courts have not granted relief under circumstances such as are alleged in this bill against the city."[4]

Another example of the protection of natural resources through the protection of property rights can be found in England and Scotland. There, in contrast to the United States, fishing rights along the banks of streams are privately owned by landowners along the streams. These rights to fish can be sold or leased, even though the water itself is not privately owned.

Owners of fishing rights can take polluters of streams to court if the pollution harms their fishing rights. Indeed, after an association of anglers won a celebrated case in the early 1950s against a government-owned utility and a private firm, it has only rarely been necessary to go to court to stop pollution that damages fishing. Once established by precedent, such rights seldom need to be defended in court unless in a particular case the circumstances are new and

---

[3]See Roger E. Meiners and Bruce Yandle, *The Common Law: How it Protects the Environment*, PERC Policy Series PS-13 (Bozeman, MT.: PERC, May 1998), 4–10.

[4]*Carmichael v. City of Texarkana*, 94 F. 561 (W.D.Ark, 1899) at 574.

unlike previous cases. When the courts are doing their job in protecting property rights, natural resources are protected more effectively than by extensive bureaucratic controls such as contemporary environmental regulations.

The tradition that protected the Carmichaels in the 19th century still protects citizens today. However, in many cases, these common-law rules have been superseded by government regulations. For example, while the Carmichaels sued a city in a different state and won, the City of Milwaukee in 1972 tried to sue the State of Illinois for polluting its water. But the passage of the Clean Water Act in 1972 led a judge to dismiss the case because water pollution was now in the hands of the federal agencies.[5]

3. Market trades and market prices bring narrow personal interest into harmony with the general welfare.

Adam Smith recognized that voluntary exchange channels individual desires, as if by an "invisible hand," into socially beneficial activities. The individual may or may not care deeply about the happiness of others in the trade, but it pays that individual to act *as if* the happiness of others matters. After all, the more that the seller can please the buyer, the more willing the buyer is to pay the price the seller wants. Similarly, if buyers can please suppliers by offering to pay more, the suppliers will be more responsive to their desires.

Each buyer and each seller may act with little knowledge of what any other person wants or needs. But market prices direct each person to satisfy the needs of others. Prices encourage producers to provide what members of society want the most, relative to their cost, and to satisfy any particular want in the least costly way. Consumers, too, are strongly influenced by market prices and they, too, act as if they care about their fellow consumers. When prices increase, they consume less; when prices decrease, they consume more. By economizing when goods are scarce, they allow more for other consumers. They purchase more when the goods are plentiful and there is a lot to go around. Actual and expected offers in the marketplace are guidance from the so-called invisible hand.

---

[5]Bruce Yandle, *Common Sense and Common Law for the Environment* (Lanham, Md.: Rowman & Littlefield, 1997), 109.

Consider energy markets. Each consumer of electricity chooses whether to use electric heat, and how high or low to set the thermostat. In addition to preferences about temperature, these decisions reflect the price of electricity. When prices are high, people will economize, making more available for others. When prices are low, they will consume more.

These decisions in turn also influence the decisions of others, even those made by other industries. For instance, individual consumer choices about electricity consumption affect how much aluminum will be produced and which producers will supply more than others.

Aluminum production requires large quantities of electricity. Higher electricity prices raise the price of aluminum compared with substitute metals and especially raise costs for producers that use a lot of electricity per ton of aluminum. Producers who conserve on the use of electricity enjoy a competitive advantage and are likely to produce a larger share of aluminum sold in the market. Thus, even with little or no knowledge of why electricity prices are rising throughout the economy, each consumer makes choices that move sales away from the expensive energy sources and toward conservation or substitute energy sources, and away from inefficient electricity producers and toward more efficient ones.

4. Private rights and market exchange minimize conflict.

Conflicts over environmental resources when they drag on and on are almost always political conflicts. Government decisions favor the side with the most political power (that is, the one with the greatest ability to influence elected officials and regulators). The losing side must accept this and usually pay taxes for the result they do not like. The political decisionmaking process is often a zero-sum game. In other words, what one person or interest group wins, another person or interest group must give up.

In contrast, market exchanges tend to be win-win. Even though there is plenty of negotiation and disagreement in the marketplace, the solutions that people agree on are ones that both parties want—at least compared with available alternatives. And a would-be buyer whose offer is rejected does not have to pay. Because market decisions are voluntary, people will not agree to an exchange unless they think it will improve their situations.

Often individuals or organizations make different decisions in the political arena than they would in the free market. This point can be illustrated by the experience of the National Audubon Society.

Audubon owns the Rainey Preserve in Louisiana, a wildlife refuge that provides nesting grounds for snowy egrets and other rare birds. Audubon allowed drilling for natural gas and oil there from the 1940s until 1999.[6]

When the potential of its energy reserves (mainly natural gas) became known, the society chose to exploit its deposits. Audubon experts and the biologists for the oil companies worked out methods of drilling and production that could be conducted without harming the snowy egrets and other birds and animals. The companies had to meet Audubon's strict stipulations; they were not allowed to drill during nesting season, for example. Audubon gave up substantial income by demanding the stipulations, but by doing so, it continued the protected status of the natural habitat.

The cooperation between the National Audubon Society and the production companies benefited both. Revenues for Audubon totaled more than $25 million over the years, helping Audubon pursue its mission, both at Rainey and elsewhere. The producers of natural gas earned revenues that would have been lost if Rainey had been closed to them.

The story is far different on land owned by the government in Alaska. The Audubon Society is adamantly opposed to oil drilling in the Arctic National Wildlife Refuge. "A wildlife refuge is no place for an oil rig!" says one of its flyers, as the organization argues vehemently that drilling would be destructive. Audubon's president claims that drilling there would be an environmental disaster.

Would it really? The fact that the government, not Audubon, owns the land means that the actual stipulations for exploration and drilling would result from a political process. Audubon might have an impact, but not the control that it has over its own preserve, nor would it receive any benefit. So it is understandable that Audubon opposes any drilling.

---

[6]For the full story of the Rainey Preserve, see John Baden and Richard Stroup, "Saving the Wilderness: A Radical Proposal," *Reason* 12 (July 1981), 28–36; Pamela Snyder and Jane S. Shaw, "PC Drilling in a Wildlife Refuge," *Wall Street Journal*, September 7, 1995; and John Flicker, "Don't Desecrate the Arctic Refuge," *Wall Street Journal*, September 18, 1995.

For the record, Audubon officials argue that the Arctic Refuge, with its cold climate and fragile tundra soil, may be less suited to drilling than the lush semitropical environment of the Rainey Preserve. This point is debatable but, in any case, it can be reasonably assumed that if Audubon owned the refuge, constructive negotiations would be conducted, with a serious search for mutually beneficial solutions. Without that search, it is unlikely that anyone can accurately predict whether or not Audubon would approve drilling if it owned the land.

As the example shows, ownership fosters cooperation. Such cooperation is important not only when something like energy development conflicts with environmental values. At other times, environmental values themselves can conflict. Here, too, markets offer tools for cooperation.

For example, how should pristine open space around a backwoods lake be used? It could be open to people from nearby cities for hiking, camping, fishing, and swimming. Or it could be closed to all visitors (except, perhaps, research biologists) to protect its rare flora and fauna. Both alternatives have merit. Some environmentalists will want one option; others, a different one. In such cases, it's hard to know what is really in the public interest.

We often witness acrimonious discussions at public meetings, read angry letters to newspaper editors, and learn of the pressures on government officials when environmental decisions are made politically. Former allies, all viewing themselves as environmentalists, take different sides depending on their own goals and the expected costs and benefits (to their own narrow goals) they face.

If the decision is made privately in the market, however, there will be little acrimony and more productive discussion. Suppose the owner of the land around the lake wants to sell it. Someone who wants it for a campground will have to determine whether the public will support a campground by paying fees. Those who want to set it aside as a wildlife preserve must determine whether they or their associates can generate the funds to purchase it. People who get involved in the bargaining and the decision have an incentive to find ways to meet their own goals at the least cost to all. If they can come up with a solution that creates more value, they can ask more (or offer less) in return.

That is why each party has a good reason to consider additional uses that may be compatible. Although each party has the right to be dogmatic, favoring only specific narrow goals, such an attitude may be costly for them, forfeiting possible opportunities to achieve many of the party's goals. The result of the negotiation could be a campground or a private nature preserve, or an innovation that allows for both.

Not everyone will get what he or she wants. Those who are not willing to provide any resources will probably be outside of the negotiations; only those who have something to offer are involved. Political decisions do not please everyone either. The key difference is that in a private setting, those who do not engage in the negotiations or whose offers are rejected do not have to pay for the outcome. In contrast, when a decision such as establishing a park is made publicly, taxpayers usually bear the costs, even those who had no say in the decision and who may not even be able to use the park.

5. Market prices provide knowledge that is complex, dispersed, and constantly updated.

Market prices provide participants information from all corners of the market, which increasingly means from all over the world. The information is in a highly condensed form. The reasons for a price rise or a price decline are not conveyed—just the vital fact of increasing or decreasing scarcity compared with other goods and services. Prices do, however, carry something else—a powerful incentive for buyers and sellers to act on the information.

Further, market prices adjust constantly to all of the supply and demand variables, providing each buyer and each seller with up-to-date information on changes in relative values in the world around them. Without market signals, it would be nearly impossible to evaluate the effect of (or even keep track of) all these bits of knowledge regarding scarcity in many uses and locations. Yet each one is relevant to the cost and the value of what is preserved, produced, and offered in the marketplace.

The value and price of logging rights in southwestern Montana, for example, depend on timber supply and lumber demands all over the globe. The same is true for the price of wheat in Kansas and the value of hunting on safari (with a gun or a camera) in South Africa. Prices change constantly, telling everyone about changing factors around the globe.

When resources are not privately owned and are traded in open markets, this vital flow of information is missing. That is the case with our national parks.[7]

Most of the funds for the national parks are tax dollars appropriated by Congress. Park visitors pay only a small fraction of the cost of the services they receive. In 1995, for example, proceeds from national park recreation fees covered only 7.5 percent of the cost of park operations. Thus, park managers have little information about how much the various services are worth to visitors. To learn what people want, they have to rely on expensive surveys and polls, which can reach only a small number of people.

Without knowing what visitors want, park managers allocate their budgets with critical information missing. Should the roads, buildings, and sewers be improved? Should more rangers be hired for interpretive programs? Should campgrounds be kept open and operating hours lengthened? Should new campgrounds be added? The Park Service cannot know the answers because a market is lacking.

Even when park managers have valid information, they may not have an incentive to use it. For example, people who stay in campgrounds in the national parks pay a large share of the operating expenses. In the summer of 1996, Yellowstone National Park managers, trying to save money, closed a campground. In fact, this campground was profitable—that is, it earned more than it cost to operate. However, the revenues from the campground went to the U.S. Treasury Department in Washington, not to the Yellowstone National Park managers. By closing the campground, the park managers reduced their expenditures, but they reduced the revenues to the Treasury by a larger amount. It would have drained their park budget to keep the campground open, even though doing so would plainly be worth more to the users than it was costing to operate.

In contrast, for owners of private campgrounds, amusement parks, museums, and other attractions that also draw visitors, information is always flowing and managers always have an incentive to respond to that information. These owners must pay for the resources they use and collect the needed revenue from customers. If people don't

[7]Donald R. Leal and Holly Lippke Fretwell, *Back to the Future to Save Our Parks*, PERC Policy Series PS-10 (Bozeman, Mont.: PERC, June 1997).

come to the museum, revenues fall. Owners must do something to attract customers who are willing to pay the full cost (or donors who will pay for them) or they will have to close their doors.

The National Park Service may be starting to realize that it needs better information and better incentives. A number of states have found that when their park systems rely on the visitors, not the state legislature, for revenues, they begin to provide services that visitors want and are willing to pay for. Now 16 state park systems rely on user fees for more than half of their operating budgets. Two systems, those in Vermont and New Hampshire, get their entire operating budgets from user fees.

Following the lead of the state parks, a federal demonstration program has raised entrance fees to the national parks and allowed the individual parks to use 80 percent of those fees rather than send them to the U.S. Treasury in Washington. Thus, the park managers directly benefit by serving the visitors. The new fees have paid for repairing roads and trails and shoring up deteriorating structures. Most visitors don't seem to mind the fees. The entrance fee is usually a small portion of a family's expenditures on a trip to the national park, so higher fees keep few people, if any, from being able to enjoy our national treasures. A survey of national park visitors found that 83 percent believe the fees were about right or were even too low.

6. Markets encourage solutions that are appropriate for specific circumstances.

The market system spurs conservation. Producers benefit when they save on resources because their costs decline. They also benefit, as do their customers, by developing new technologies that increase the value of the output from the resources they use.

But proper resource conservation differs from one place to another and from one time to another. An excellent solution to a problem in one situation may not work well for a seemingly similar problem in a different setting.

Consider the question of cloth versus disposable diapers. Although cloth diapers have the advantage of being used again and again, they must be washed and dried each time. That requires hot water and detergent, disposal of waste water, and perhaps heat to dry the diapers. In addition, if a diaper service is used with its

29

efficient machinery and labor, transportation to and from the customer also places a demand on the environment.

Disposable diapers are used only once. Each new diaper is produced in a manufacturing process that requires new cellulose fiber and plastic liners, and disposal requires transportation and space in a landfill.

In a place where water and the energy to heat it are scarce but landfill space is plentiful—the rural West, for example—disposable diapers may be better for the environment. But where landfill space is scarcer and more expensive but water is abundant—urban areas in the East, for example—cloth diapers may be environmentally better.

If those who make and those who buy diapers pay the full cost of their use, market prices will automatically signal the relative resource costs for the specific situation. Higher water prices signal scarce supply that makes water conservation more valuable. This encourages the use of disposable diapers. The price signal not only gives information, it also encourages users to choose the product that, under their specific circumstances, places less total cost, including environmental costs, on society.[8]

Thus, the market system rewards conservation of the more highly valued resources. However, it does so only if producers, consumers, and third parties are secure against polluters. If nonconsumers suffer air pollution from diaper-service trucks that travel to and from their customers' homes, then the consumers are not paying the full cost of cloth diapers, and the market signal to the producer is distorted. Similarly, if landfills are too cheap (that is, if the full cost of maintaining them is not being paid by those who use them), consumers may be getting an incorrect market signal.

7. Private ownership provides freedom and a powerful incentive to innovate.

Over the past century, new technology has led to less pollution and to the use of fewer raw materials per unit of output. This has been true for steel mills (once fiery behemoths belching smoke but

---

[8]Mark Duda and Jane S. Shaw, *A New Environmental Tool? Assessing Life Cycle Assessment*, Contemporary Issues Series 81 (St. Louis, Mo.: Center for the Study of American Business, August 1996).

Figure 2-2
ENERGY USE PER PRODUCT DECLINES IN THE UNITED STATES

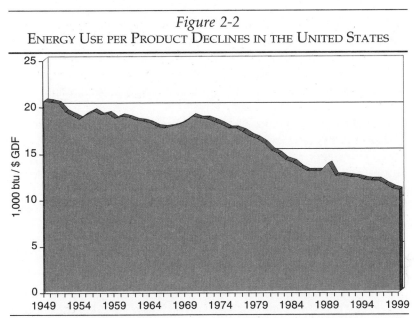

SOURCE: Steven Hayward, Index of Leading Environmental Indicators. (San Francisco: Pacific Research Institute, April 2001), citing Energy Information Administration Statistics, p. 57.

now relatively clean, with many using scrap steel as their raw materials) as well as for aluminum cans (which over time have been engineered to become thinner and thinner). Similarly, new technology has reduced the amount of energy required to produce a specific amount of output (Figure 2-2). Innovation is largely beneficial not only to manufacturers and users, but also to the environment.

Innovation is essential to progress, but it means change, and change is always difficult. It is usually easier to continue doing something the way it has always been done. A market society encourages innovation, but also keeps it within limits.

To have an incentive to innovate, an entrepreneur must be able to benefit personally from a change. This incentive comes through ownership. An owner or an investor can save money by new techniques that reduce the use of resources. Owners can earn more revenues with new or better products. At the same time, they don't want to lose all of their wealth in a reckless pursuit of profits, so they are cautious about pursuing zany ideas and will abandon those that prove unworkable. In a private system, the individual's wealth, not society's, is at stake. Other people do not pay for innovations that go awry.

Innovation is so embedded in a market system that it may be hard to imagine a system without it. However, the socialist economies of Eastern Europe were, by and large, such a system. The Trabant automobile, produced in East Germany between 1959 and 1989, illustrates what happens without innovation.

In those years, central planners ran East Germany, and private property rights were largely missing from the economic scene. Managers had little incentive to innovate and little freedom to act at all. Production plans were dictated by central planners, and managers were mainly rewarded for meeting quantitative output goals.

It wasn't until after the Berlin Wall came down in 1989 that many Americans saw the Trabant. An American auto magazine, *Car and Driver*, brought the Trabant over to have a look at it. On the positive side, the editors reported that the car provided basic transportation and was easy to fix (similar things were said about the Model T Fords in the early 20th century). But its top speed was 66 miles per hour, it was noisy, and, the editors said, it had "no discernible handling." It spewed "a plume of oil and gray exhaust smoke" and didn't have a gas gauge. In fact, the Trabant's exhaust was so noxious that the Environmental Protection Agency refused to let the *Car and Driver* staff drive it on public streets.[9]

The Trabant was backward, dirty, and inefficient because its design was the same as when it was first manufactured in 1959. The last model had been introduced in 1964 and since market pressures were absent, there had been no technological change. In contrast, the Volkswagen, the "people's car" of West Germany during the same years, was continually updated. By 1989, it was efficient and caused little pollution. Pollution control laws were a factor in reducing emissions, but fuel economy and performance alone would have brought some of the reduction. The safety, comfort, performance, and pollution control of the VW changed constantly for the better, while the Trabant stagnated.

[9]Rich Ceppos, "The Car Who Came In from the Cold," *Car and Driver*, December 1990, 89–97.

8. Markets foster a variety of plans and actions, allowing unusual creative ideas to be tested.

In a market system, many mistakes are made. Entrepreneurs come up with new products and customers reject some of them. Entrepreneurs try to save money by innovations and some of the innovations don't work. In the United States, in fact, about 1 newly incorporated business in 10 fails each year.

But the ideas that do work, the products that do sell, the businesses that do succeed provide the change that over the years transforms the economy and increases wealth.

Change occurs rapidly in a market system because individuals don't need consensus or majority approval to pursue their ideas, as they would if their ideas had to be adopted by a democratic political process. As long as people don't harm others, they can test their innovations, and in a market, "the early bird gets the worm." Successful innovators earn temporary profits, while others must adopt the innovations that work later just to survive in business.

History is replete with examples of people who have challenged the conventional wisdom. In the 1970s, it looked as though computers would be ever increasing in size and complexity, but a few hobbyists had a different idea. Some innovators put together a crude computer and began selling it as an assemble-it-yourself kit through *Popular Science* magazine. They created the first personal computer, revolutionizing the future of computers and to a large extent changing the way people conduct business and leisure activities.

Such innovations occur in the environmental realm as well, often long before public policy recognizes the need for change. The story of the Hawk Mountain Sanctuary in eastern Pennsylvania is an example.

Hawk Mountain is a ridge that lies along a natural migration route for hawks. In the early 1930s, hunters came to Hawk Mountain from miles around to shoot hawks. At the time, not only was hunting hawks popular, but the biological experts thought that hawks, like other predatory birds, were undesirable and not worth preserving. In fact, the state paid a bounty to those who killed a certain kind of hawk.

Rosalie Edge, a conservationist and activist, opposed the wholesale slaughter of hawks. She tried to convince biologists, state officials, and leaders of the National Audubon Society that hawks have a rightful place in nature and should not be eradicated. Her efforts at persuasion failed, but then she took a different tack. In 1934, she and some friends came up with enough money to buy an option on Hawk Mountain, and later they bought the mountain. She created a sanctuary for the hawks, forbidding hunts there. Today the 2,000-acre reserve is a prime bird-watching location.

Edge's view that hawks have an important place in nature is now conventional wisdom. It is easy to forget that this idea was radical 60 years ago. Only because Hawk Mountain was privately owned could Edge exercise her vision of wildlife protection.

The private nonprofit sector has historically been a key component of conservation efforts. Starting late in the 19th century, for example, the National Audubon Society was formed to save birds like the snowy egret, which was endangered because women's hats were decorated with their plumes. In addition to campaigning against wearing such feathers and trying to change some laws, the Audubon Society began to purchase or accept by donation natural areas that would become wildlife preserves. Today, Audubon has 100 wildlife sanctuaries and nature centers around the country. More recently, the Delta Waterfowl Foundation has paid farmers in the United States and Canada to protect nesting areas for ducks and geese on their farmlands. Among the most famous of the organizations that protect endangered species and preserve open space is the Nature Conservancy. Donations by individuals and corporations provide it with the funds to purchase land and create preserves. Indeed, around the country large numbers of private, nonprofit organizations called land trusts have sprung up to maintain land in a more or less natural state.

9. Private ownership makes resource owners accountable to the future.

People sometimes assume that a private owner has little incentive to protect a resource for the future and may be quite willing to destroy its long-term value for short-term gain. Only the government can truly preserve a natural resource, this line of reasoning goes, because the government, unlike the private sector, plans for the long run. This common assumption, however, is largely false.

The price of land reflects the future benefits that the owner expects to receive from that land. In economists' language, today's price is the capitalized value of the future stream of benefits (net of the costs required to protect or produce those benefits). In other words, the current price incorporates the stream of benefits that are expected in the future.

Just as prices convey information about changing demand and supply all over the globe, a capital market—the buying and selling of capital assets such as land, buildings, bonds, or even corporate stock certificates—allows the voice of future buyers to speak today through current market bids for ownership. The operation of the capital market sends price signals about the use of capital assets such as land. Those few people who first see that a resource will rise in value can profit by buying and preserving it, and selling at a higher price when others recognize its value. Even a shortsighted owner who is personally concerned only with the present will respond to these signals because they change the *current* value of his or her assets. Of course, the owner can ignore the price signals, but then he or she must deal with the resulting reduction in wealth.

In a sense, the value of a resource is a hostage that ensures protection and good management by the owner. This value gives the owner an incentive to maintain the land's productivity and, where possible, to make investments that improve it. If the land is damaged, its value declines whether the damage occurs through misuse, negligence, trespass, or pollution. If necessary, an owner will go to court against trespassers or polluters to protect the value of the property.

The incentive to look to the future is clear for conventional sources of income such as agricultural crops or housing developments. But it also holds true for goods of an environmental nature.

Consider television magnate Ted Turner. After a successful and innovative career, he began buying ranches in the West and Southwest. On the Flying D Ranch, south of Bozeman, Montana, for example, he decided not to raise traditional livestock but instead to manage the ranch largely for bison and elk. To do this, he decided to increase the number of trophy animals over time. In 1999 he was able to charge elk hunters as much as $9,500 per hunt. For additional fees, hunters can also take deer and bison during their hunts. However, there are also hunts that cost much less.

In all, the ranch is earning roughly $300,000 in additional revenue per year. This added revenue stream has raised the value of the ranch. It also leads Turner to manage the ranch in a way that is pleasing to hunters and encourages the proliferation of diverse wild-life, not just elk, deer, and bison.[10]

10. It is costly to establish and maintain private rights.

Private property rights benefit both the individual and society, but not everything is privately owned. One reason is that sometimes defining and defending property rights is extremely expensive. Thus, at times a resource isn't valuable enough for anyone to make the effort.

Looking back over American history, for example, we notice that while the first colonists in New England established settlements where they lived, they made no effort to own the surrounding wilderness. It was full of wild beasts and inhabited by sometimes hostile Indians. It offered nothing useful for them.

Over time, that view of the wilderness changed. As the Eastern settlements became more crowded, wilderness became more attractive. Settlers also had more tools than before (better guns and better saws, for example) so they could hunt, log, and live more safely in the forests. They began to establish ownership.

Today, of course, many people have a very different view of wilderness. For them, it is something to be prized, a place to get away from urban crowds and to commune with nature. That is why many Americans encouraged the federal government to set aside large areas as wilderness and why individual Americans frequently try to buy a little piece of wilderness as a retirement or summer home. Over time, wilderness changed from a worthless danger to a valuable resource.

Similarly, when American pioneers reached the arid western territories, the prairies and grasslands were so vast that no one even thought about owning them. Cattle roamed where buffalo had once wandered in giant herds. At first, there were so few cattle compared to the vast rangeland that they caused no problem.

Eventually that changed. Cattle became numerous enough that owners needed to separate one herd from another. Had they been in the East, they would have used wooden fences, but in much of the West that was impossible. There was less wood to build fences

---

[10]Terry L. Anderson and Donald R. Leal, *Enviro-Capitalists: Doing Good While Doing Well* (Lanham, Md.: Rowman & Littlefield, 1997), 75–77.

with, and the areas that had to be fenced stretched over square miles, not mere acres. As the value of separating the herds increased, ranchers began to experiment. They organized crews of cowboys to round up the herds and they began creating distinctive brands for their cattle.

And then some entrepreneurs invented barbed wire. Barbed wire is effective and, compared with wood fences in large parts of the arid West, it is cheap. The invention of barbed wire reduced the cost of establishing property rights to herds of livestock and to the lands they grazed. Barbed wire allowed for the effective defense of property rights, a defense that had been missing.

When a resource is not valued highly enough to justify the cost of establishing and defending property rights, the resource may not be privately owned. Over time, however, this situation can change. The value can increase and the cost of protecting rights may go down.

To see a relatively recent change in property rights, we have only to look at ranches in the western United States. Early in the nation's history, no wildlife was owned. Any person with a gun had access to wildlife, and excessive hunting occurred. The passenger pigeon, which was so abundant in the 19th century that no one ever imagined it might disappear, became officially extinct in 1914 because there were no controls on hunting it.

However, as the game birds became scarcer, hunters and others put increasing pressure on the government to control the hunters' access to wildlife. State governments, which were viewed as being responsible for wildlife, established and enforced hunting seasons and bag limits.

More recently, private ownership of wildlife has increased. As hunting on public lands becomes more widespread, private landowners have found that they can use laws against trespassers to control access to their lands for hunting. Hunters are increasingly willing to pay for quality hunting (as Turner's experience with hunting on his Montana ranch indicates). The value of hunting has increased, and ranchers are responding by managing their lands to conserve more wildlife.

The value of water in streams and rivers has also increased. In the second half of the 19th century when western water law developed, the chief demand for water was to divert it—take it out of streams—for irrigation or other purposes. But in recent years, many people have wanted water left in the streams to protect the fish and to allow recreational use of the streams. As the value of water kept in the streams has risen, these instream flows have led environmental groups and fishing associations to effect legal changes that allow them to privately define, defend, and transfer the rights to those flows. The law has begun to allow the treatment of instream flows as private property, just as irrigators have for many decades been able to treat their rights to divert water from the streams as private property.

Conclusion

This chapter has shown that when property rights are defined, defendable, and divestible, markets turn the conflict that is caused by scarcity into a cooperative search for mutual benefits by buyers and sellers. However, property rights are not always three-D. When they are not, environmental problems can arise.

3. Coercion: Protecting the Environment with Government Action

Newspaper headlines are full of conflicts over environmental issues. Should the government allow exploration for oil in the Arctic National Wildlife Refuge? How much sulfur dioxide should power plants be allowed to emit? Should the pesticide DDT be used to attack malaria-bearing mosquitoes?

In these cases as in many others, the cooperative spirit illustrated by market transactions in Chapter 2 is missing. It has been replaced by anger and stubborn positions taken by both sides. In each of these cases, the coercive power of government contributes to the conflict.

Yes, governments have a critical role in protecting the environment. The problem is that often the government intervenes in ways far different from this critical role.

The government has a legal right to use force. Thus, on the positive side, it can police the protection of rights and prevent violence or fraud by one person or group against another, including rights against harm from pollution. In addition to having these police powers, the government protects rights by recording claims such as records of ownership and sales of land and water rights. These activities help markets function better by reducing poaching of property rights. For example, such records help to more easily identify the owner of property that is the source of harmful activity. As noted in Chapter 2, property rights, when properly defined and defended, can further environmental goals.

Other ways that governments intervene, however, are not so consistently beneficial. The government can own and manage resources such as land, wildlife, and water. It can also control how people and companies use resources, replacing market decisions with political decisions, as it does frequently with environmental issues.

Political decisions often lead to clashes because individuals in government have different incentives from those who buy and sell in markets. Environmental statutes typically state specific goals, and direct agency officials to use their authority to achieve them. In contrast, market participants must obtain cooperation voluntarily; they choose their own goals and priorities and rely on the government only for the rules and processes for settling disputes. These situations provide different incentives.

The two settings also provide different kinds of information. Markets continuously provide both buyers and sellers with market signals, primarily in the form of prices, telling them how they can do well by providing something that others want. The signals are frequent and finely tuned (in dollars and cents). Government officials, too, obtain signals. In a democracy, the signals come from the voters in elections. However, unlike markets, the signals from the voters are infrequent and seldom specific. Exactly what mandate does a newly elected official have on a specific environmental question? Unless the answer to that question was the major factor causing voters to distinguish between candidates, it is hard to say from the election outcome exactly what voters want. Most voting is by candidate, not by issue.

This chapter explains how the government obtains information, what incentives its decisionmakers face, and predictable ways that the government acts when it seeks to control resource use and environmental quality. This information illustrates the strengths and weaknesses of government and helps explain the results, both environmental and social, that we can expect from the political process.

1. Government plays a critical role in protecting individuals' rights to hold and use their properties and to be free from harms caused by others.

Governments give formal recognition to property rights, which are traded in markets. Markets are everywhere. From stock exchanges, where billions of dollars' worth of ownership interest in capital are traded daily, to the farmers' markets that appear each summer along country roads, trade is a fact of life that benefits in some way all who participate. Governments facilitate these exchanges. Governments use force (and more often the threat of force) to prevent theft and fraud. When people are confident that what they own is not going to be taken from them, they are more willing to buy and sell and to produce goods in the first place.

The economist Hernando de Soto discovered the critical role of protection of property rights when he studied the informal economy in Peru. He found that the Peruvian government, through neglect, bureaucratic inertia, and protection of privilege, had made it impossible for many Peruvians to open businesses. Entrepreneurs had to go through labyrinthine approval processes that were costly, full of detailed requirements, and nearly impossible to complete. Thus, many people in the poorer sectors had to operate their enterprises illegally if they were to have businesses at all. As a result, they did not have the basic protection of property rights that we generally expect government to provide. De Soto concluded that if society is to be cooperative and productive, property rights must be formally recognized so that people can plan for the future, knowing that they can keep what they earn and that any investment they make will not be taken away from them.[1]

Governments rarely create property rights. Although the history of property rights varies from place to place, property rights are usually established informally when land or other natural resources become valuable enough for individuals to work with them. Later, these informal rights are confirmed or codified by a governmental entity.

The discovery of gold in California in 1848 illustrates this process. The sudden increase in the value of land led briefly to conflicts among California miners. But soon the miners began to make agreements about how the land and the veins of gold would be divided. Claimants worked mines together, having made contracts spelling out how any finds would be allocated. They did this even though there was no effective government in those areas at the time. Later, when the federal government came West, it formalized the rights and provided legal protection.

Throughout most of the history of the United States, the government's role with respect to land and water was primarily to recognize, record, and protect individual property rights. While the U.S. government claimed ownership to large amounts of land, most of it was gradually settled and became privately owned through various laws such as the Homestead Act of 1862. (This policy of divestiture

---

[1] Hernando de Soto, *The Mystery of Capital* (New York: Basic Books, 2000).

41

or privatization ended late in the 19th century, when the federal government decided to keep many western lands.)

Once land was privately owned, state governments provided common-law courts; that is, civil courts through which people decided disputes. Among those disputes were issues over damage from pollution, as discussed in Chapter 2. By enforcing property rights, government courts protected people from excessive pollution, just as they protected individuals from theft and from personal assault.

Protection against polluters depends on the plaintiffs' ability to show that harm is occurring or is imminent. That is easier than gaining a conviction against a criminal offense, which requires proof beyond a reasonable doubt, but even so, it can be difficult to prove. In some cases, there may not be sufficient evidence that the pollution was caused by the person or entity charged. Or the extent of harm may not be clear. Often there is a lag between the pollution and harm, as when groundwater contamination shows up long after a leak has occurred. And often there is much scientific uncertainty about the effects on human health of differing levels of pollution.

So although Americans have the right not to be seriously harmed by polluters, the knowledge needed to demonstrate the harm effectively may be lacking. In addition, some important environmental concerns don't lend themselves to private suits conducted under common law. Although the residents downwind from industrial polluters such as the Asarco smelters in Ruston, Washington, and Helena, Montana, were successful in suing the firm for harm from sulfur dioxide pollution, that form of recourse is not manageable for those who suffer from smog in the Los Angeles basin. Smog there is caused by millions of scattered polluters, especially cars, and there are millions of scattered smog victims.

To act under common law, there needs to be a single harmed individual, or relatively few such individuals, who have the ability and the incentive to protect themselves through the courts. Similarly, it is important that specific identifiable polluters can be brought to court. There does not seem to be a way that common-law protection of property rights will be a reasonable or effective solution for the many millions of people who are both victims and perpetrators of the harm. In cases like this, if the government is to protect its citizens and their property against invasions and harms from others, including polluters, it must sometimes regulate more directly.

Partly because of these problems, a shift occurred in the second half of the 20th century. Dissatisfaction with the way the courts handled pollution problems began to develop. Undoubtedly, this also happened because people became more alarmed about pollution. The nation was getting wealthier and people had food on their tables. They looked around and saw pollution that bothered them more than it had bothered their parents and grandparents. From relying primarily on courts for protection against pollution, the nation moved to direct governmental regulation of polluting activities.

2. Direct regulation of polluting activities bypasses—but does not eliminate—the problem of missing information.

Property rights protected in common-law courts are clearly imperfect solutions to the problems of pollution. Critics pointed out that the courts were slow and the outcome uncertain. Without better scientific data, the courts were not well-equipped to deal with pollution that might cause illnesses such as cancer, which can be triggered at one point in time but not actually appear until many years later. Further, the link between chemical exposures and disease might be based on probability, not on a clear linkage. Knowledge and proof of cause and effect would be difficult to establish.

Beginning in the 1970s, Congress passed a series of environmental laws that gave federal agencies sweeping powers to directly control activities that might have environmental consequences. The early 1970s were full of new laws, from the Clean Air Act and the National Environmental Policy Act passed in 1970 to the Clean Water Act of 1972, the Endangered Species Act of 1973, and both the Toxic Substances Control Act and the Resource Conservation and Recovery Act of 1976. In 1980, the Superfund law designed to clean up hazardous waste dumps was adopted.

Standards were set. Were they too tight or too lax? Would the best standard be different in different areas? Technologies are often specified in the regulations formed under such laws. Were they the right ones? Will they continue to be the right ones? Answering any of these questions requires information of the same kinds that courts would need to address the same problems. Yet the information is not necessarily produced. In fact, a government agency may have little interest in gaining objective answers to the questions. Rather, the officials may prefer more and tighter regulations.

As a result of these laws, the mushrooming power of federal regulatory agencies, especially the Environmental Protection Agency, helped to reduce certain pollution problems. Environmental laws have had the strong support of most citizens, and environmental activists became more influential as their claims warned of large and imminent dangers, ranging from acid rain to global warming. Their fund-raising letters were especially vivid, proving to be a valuable fund-raising tool. More and more stringent regulations were adopted. At the same time, the costs imposed on taxpayers and on those forced to comply with regulations also mushroomed.

Despite some early successes, many of the costly regulations, when closely examined by economists and other policy analysts, did not appear to yield large benefits. They were popular with a frightened public, but when better information was produced, the benefits often appeared to be much smaller than had been expected, both because the dangers had been exaggerated and because the solutions did not necessarily work as intended.

EPA programs such as Superfund and toxic substances control allowed government officials to pursue narrow goals without taking into account competing goals or having to provide the kind of cause-and-effect information required in the courts. The result was costly programs that produced little in the way of demonstrable benefits.

That led to something of a backlash. Some citizens who were directly affected strongly opposed specific regulations when costs were high and when large reduction in harms from the regulations could not be demonstrated. Much of the period after 1970 has been characterized by hostile confrontations. On the one side, environmental activists press for tougher regulations; on the other side, the companies and individuals who most obviously bear the burden of those regulations resist. Of course, many of us pay for inefficient regulation without realizing that the cost of what we buy and what we do is greater, with little benefit in return, because of those regulations.

3. Decisionmakers in government agencies often fail to see the big picture; good intentions can lead to bad results.

It is true that markets are imperfect and governments can sometimes solve specific problems. But government programs often end up helping organized and active political and bureaucratic constituencies (that is, special interests) rather than solving a particular problem in the broad interest of the unorganized general public. There are several reasons for this. One can be summarized as tunnel vision. This is the term Supreme Court Justice Stephen Breyer applied to the federal regulators, including the EPA.[2]

For Breyer, tunnel vision is the tendency of government employees to focus exclusively on the objectives of their agencies, or even the specific programs within their agencies, at the expense of all other concerns. As noted earlier, all people have narrow goals. Narrow goals lead to tunnel vision if the legislators writing the law state strong goals but do not provide guidance to the agency implementing the law. The benefits of tighter regulations should be balanced against the sacrifice of resources, or the production forgone, that occurs to comply with stricter regulations. Without such guidance— which would force elected officials to make difficult decisions—the real costs that regulations impose may never enter the thinking of agency officials.

In contrast to regulators who sometimes have expansive authority under vague laws, market participants can only regulate in two ways. The first is to show in court that actions harming them are violating their rights, and that the court should halt the harmful actions, require the cleanup, or insist that damages be paid. The second way is to offer something in exchange to those they are asking to make sacrifices.

But a regulator can write very strict and costly standards under some environmental laws with only a plausible report about potential risks or potential gains. No proof of claimed risks or claimed benefits is necessary and no review of their decisions is possible, so long as they cannot be proven to have acted in an arbitrary or capricious fashion.

Not surprisingly, tunnel vision sometimes leads to excessive regulation that may cause more harm than good. The 1980 Comprehensive Environmental Response Compensation and Liability Act, known as Superfund, is an example. The law created a large fund of tax money for cleaning up abandoned waste sites. The fund came

---

[2]Stephen Breyer, *Breaking the Vicious Circle: Toward Effective Risk Regulation* (Cambridge, Mass.: Harvard University Press, 1993), 11–19.

initially from a tax on chemical-producing industries, but the EPA was authorized to obtain compensation from any individual or company that it could show had deposited any hazardous waste in the site. To obtain this compensation, EPA officials have no responsibility to show wrongdoing or any real damage to others or even any real and present risk emanating from the site.

Superfund was aimed at a genuine problem. Buried wastes have sometimes leaked from their underground sites and caused harm. If no owner responsible for the wastes was found who could be sued and forced to clean up and compensate those harmed, Superfund was supposed to be able to get the job done.

The Love Canal waste site in Niagara Falls in upstate New York spurred passage of the law. Chemicals from the site had leaked into the yards and basements of nearby residents, creating unsightly messes and bringing unwanted smells. And much worse was feared. Two hastily written health studies suggested that diseases and birth defects might have resulted from the leaking chemicals. The fact that the studies were discredited was hardly noticed in the uproar.

The Love Canal event galvanized Congress. Noting that the courts had not been able to bring swift, sure, low-cost relief to those who feared injury from chemicals leaking from underground storage sites, Congress passed the Superfund law. President Jimmy Carter, in the last weeks of his presidency, signed it.

But Superfund did not prove to be the swift, sure, low-cost solution that people wanted. It was supposed to cost at most a few billion dollars and be paid for mainly by those whose pollution had caused serious harms or risks. But that was not the result.

In the first 12 years after Superfund was established, the program spent $20 billion, and its costs grew along with delays in its cleanups of hazardous waste sites. Despite the expenditures, the program showed little gain in the way of human health benefits. In their 1996 study, *Calculating Risks*, researchers James T. Hamilton and W. Kip Viscusi reported a number of discouraging findings.[3] Among them—

- Most assessed Superfund risks do not pose a threat to human health now; they might do so in the future, but only if people

[3]James T. Hamilton and W. Kip Viscusi, *Calculating Risks* (Cambridge, Mass.: MIT Press, 1996).

violate commonsense precautions and actually inhabit contaminated sites, while disregarding known risks there.

- Even if exposure did occur, there is less than a 1 percent chance that the risks are as great as EPA estimates, because of the compounding of extreme assumptions made by the EPA.
- Cancer risk is the main concern at Superfund sites, because it has a long latency period and some contaminants at the sites can cause cancer in high-dose exposures. Yet at most of the sites, each cleanup is expected to avert only one-tenth of one case of cancer. Without any cleanup, only 10 of the 150 sites studied were estimated to have 1 or more expected cases.
- The average cleanup cost per site in the study was $26 million (in 1993 dollars).
- Replacing extreme EPA assumptions with more reasonable ones brought the estimated median cost per cancer case averted to more than $7 billion. At 87 of the 96 sites having the necessary data available, the costs per cancer case averted (only some of which would mean a life saved) was more than $100 million.
- Other federal programs commonly consider a life saved to be worth about $5 million. Diverting expenditures from most Superfund sites to other sites or other risk-reduction missions could save many more lives or save the same number of lives at far less cost.

This is a clear case of tunnel vision. EPA site managers have little reason to worry about whether, in forcing others to spend more money at Superfund sites to reduce environmental risks there, other important social goals consequently receive less money. Agency and program officials have pushed cleanups beyond the efficient point. Hamilton and Viscusi estimate that 95 percent of Superfund expenditures are directed at the last 0.5 percent of the risk. As President Bill Clinton said in 1993, "Superfund has been a disaster" (*Los Angeles Times*, May 10). Most observers agree. In fact, many people touched by the program are harmed rather than helped. A designated Superfund site causes property values to fall. Residents may be forced to move away, at least temporarily. People may be badly frightened for no good reason.

The firms required to pay for the cleanups have little chance to defend themselves against being billed for enormous sums. The EPA doesn't even have to prove that there is a health risk at the site, but only to show the possibility of a risk. Because Superfund established enormous potential liability for any link to ownership or control of sites that might have hazardous waste, investors and banks often refuse to lend money to develop industrial sites that might have such Superfund liability attached to them. They reject these brown-fields for untouched greenfields in the suburbs, pushing industrial and commercial development far from the inner-city people who need jobs, and often beyond the boundaries of cities that need a tax base. Once again, good intentions have had unanticipated and unwanted results.

When agencies like the EPA have the authority to make demands that they do not have to pay for and do not have to justify, efficient decisions are unlikely. Other agencies also face the same temptation—to put enormous demands on the private sector simply because tunnel vision tells them to do so and no budget restraints hold them back.

Even agencies with severe budget restraints can overcome them and are tempted to do so by tunnel vision. Their administrators will use their expertise, their control of information about programs, and often their monopoly position to push for a greater budget so that they can pursue their mission. For example, the National Park Service has often used what observers call the Washington Monument strategy.

The strategy goes like this: When the federal budget is being formulated, the National Park Service (like other bureaus and agencies) usually proposes a large increase, which then is trimmed by the Secretary of the Interior, the Office of Management and Budget, or the relevant congressional committee. The agency's budget, at least in recent times, has always been augmented, but the increase is always smaller than the Park Service would like. One response by the Park Service has been to announce that it may have to economize by shortening the hours that it can operate the Washington Monument or certain other of their most popular attractions.

The strategy tends to increase the Park Service budget. The threat of long lines of citizens (voters) waiting to get in, or outrage at not being able to enter, often persuades political appointees in the OMB or congressional committees to increase funding. In effect, Park Service leaders are saying, "Give us what we asked for or we will cut back on our most popular services."

Private firms rarely use this strategy or anything like it. Can you imagine Wal-Mart coping with lower revenues by reducing its services, dropping its most popular product lines, and shortening the hours of its most popular stores—and then advertising that this will continue until customers give them more business? A firm competing for customers has to recognize that customers always have other options. If a firm serves customers poorly, few will return and revenues will decline further. If Wal-Mart really must cut back, it would begin by dropping the least popular items, not the most popular ones. This is exactly the opposite strategy from that of a government agency like the Park Service. The agency knows that Congress must respond to complaints from voters and that taxpayers must pay any increased taxes that Congress might levy to increase the agency's budget.

Every agency is doing something similar to compete in the budget process, and most are working with sympathetic congressional committees. So while competition for budget funds is great, the upward pressure on the total budget also is strong. The Washington Monument strategy would not work if the Park Service were depending on user fees for its revenues. In that case, shortening the hours at the most popular visitor sites would reduce revenue more than shortening hours at the least popular sites. A private store facing budget problems, of course, would cut its least popular store hours, not the most popular ones.

Government regulation is imperfect. However, this does not imply that government should never act beyond the protection of property rights by common law. Instead, it means that when we turn to government to address environmental issues, we should expect to encounter problems as well as hoped-for solutions.

4. It is understandable that the individual voter may be uninformed about most policy matters and even about elected representatives.

By and large, voters do not monitor and correct the problems of government control. There is a reason why voters, who are often intelligent and well-intentioned, remain ignorant about the issues and therefore are not successful in monitoring their elected representatives.

Voters seldom decide policy issues directly. Instead, they vote for political candidates who compete to become their elected representatives and make those decisions. Voter impact is primarily at the ballot box. Unfortunately, voters frequently lack the detailed information needed to cast their ballots in a truly knowledgeable fashion.

In most elections, the choice made by a single voter is seldom decisive. Voters know this. Recognizing that the outcome will not depend on one vote, the individual voter has little incentive to spend time and effort gathering information on issues and candidates in order to cast a more informed vote. This explains why most Americans of voting age cannot name their congressional representatives even after they are elected, much less identify, understand, and compare the positions of candidates on environmental issues—or most other issues—most of the time.

To grasp in a more personal way why citizens are likely to make better-informed decisions as consumers than as voters, imagine that you are planning to buy a car next week and also to vote for one of two candidates for the U.S. Senate. You have narrowed your car choice to either a Ford Taurus or a Honda Accord. In the voting booth, you will choose between candidates Sam Smith and John Jones. Both the car purchase and the Senate vote involve complex trade-offs for you. The two cars come with many options, and you must choose among dozens of different combinations; the winning Senate candidate will represent you on hundreds of issues, although you are limited to voting for one of the two choices.

Which of these complex decisions will command more of your scarce time for research and thinking about the best choice? Since your car choice is entirely yours and you must pay the entire cost of what you choose, an uninformed car purchase could be very costly for you. But if you mistakenly vote for the wrong candidate out of ignorance, the probability is nearly zero that your vote will decide the election. Your individual vote cannot control who will actually win. Cumulatively, your vote and those of all the other people in your state will decide the election, but your choice will not. You recognize that a mistake or poorly informed choice will have little consequence on the actual outcome.

It would not be surprising, then, if you spent substantial time considering the car purchase and little time becoming informed about either the candidates or the political issues. Automobile choices are not perfectly informed decisions, but the buyer is certain to benefit from giving careful consideration to the alternatives. As a result, automakers are probably guided by better-informed votes (dollar votes, that is) than the U.S. Senate, even though decisions made by the Senate are far more important for the nation as a whole than automobile choices.

The fact that voters have little incentive to study issues and candidates carefully has enormous ramifications. First, they will rely mainly on headlines in newspapers and brief, sound-bite-length television reports, paid political advertising, and other information they can pick up casually. As consumers of news, voters discourage the media from spending time and space on the detailed and complicated information that would be necessary for them to make informed decisions. What sells well on television and in the newspapers are the human-interest stories about villains and heroes with dramatic images of shocking, high-risk situations. That is what happened in the news descriptions of Love Canal. The reports from public health officials over the following days and weeks indicating that the research reports were fundamentally flawed received little attention. To this day, a great many citizens believe that the chemical leaks at Love Canal caused severe public health effects, even though there is no credible evidence that it is true.[4]

This kind of ignorance lays the foundation for laws that attack villains and have high-sounding goals. Once the laws are implemented, the voter has turned to other matters, especially since the details are complex and not very interesting. The ignorance of the voter explains why Superfund was popular when it was passed, why most voters know little about the program's problems, and why the voters have not successfully demanded that their elected politicians eliminate the problems. This ignorance is duplicated in many environmental issues.

5. Government has no capital market, so it lacks the signals and the incentives associated with market decisions.

As noted earlier, decisions made by private firms are evaluated in the private sector's capital market. Because such a capital market is

---

[4]See Aaron Wildavsky with Michelle Malkin, "Love Canal: Was There Evidence of Harm?" in Aaron Wildavsky, *But Is It True?* (Cambridge, Mass.: Harvard University Press, 1995), 126–52.

missing, government officials do not receive correct and persuasive signals about whether its management is sound or not.

In a private market, when investors view a management decision as a good one, they keep their stock or buy more, anticipating that the value of the firm will rise. If many investors begin to think this way, their decisions lead the stock's price to rise, making its shareholders instantly more wealthy. Similarly, poor decisions lead shareholders to sell the stock and the price tends to fall. Managers respond to these capital market signals about the fluctuating value of their stock. Those who do not are likely to be replaced by owners of the stock.

Government managers do not get capital market signals. This causes numerous difficulties but poses a special problem because the federal government owns about one-third of the land mass of the United States. In other words, the government has enormous capital assets but it does not get any guidance from capital markets on whether it is managing those properties well. Government forests, grasslands, wildlife preserves, parks, and other resources (including government buildings) are seldom sold, so there is no resource price established for government assets through market trades as there is for resources in the private sector. Changes in government policy or events such as forest fires do change the value of a government-owned resource, but the changes are not reflected in any market price.

Further, unlike investors in the private sector, few individuals have a strong financial incentive to learn what is happening with the management of the resource. Because the assets can't be sold, no one benefits directly from knowing about management changes. So there is no feedback to decisionmakers from resource price changes of the kind that private owners and managers receive. When an owner or manager in the private sector takes actions that affect the resource value, the market value changes. Government agencies operate without such information and without the system of rewards and penalties that a market for capital assets passes along to private decisionmakers. These give signals and incentives to properly plan for the firm's future, even at the expense of today's profits or dividend payouts.

6. Special interest groups try to use the government's resources and regulatory authority to further their own narrow purposes.

By its very nature—because it has the power through taxing and spending and through regulation to coerce people to take actions, and because it does not depend on choice—government is called upon to take from some to give help to others. A government decision often generates substantial personal benefits for a small number of constituents while imposing a small individual cost on a large number of other voters. The big benefits to the smallest number of recipients provides them with an incentive to lobby hard. Yet the rational ignorance of the voter means that the largest number who pay the costs know nothing, or almost nothing, about it.

The federal government's program to supply below-cost water to farmers in the arid West illustrates this imbalance. Using the Central Utah Project's dams and canals, the federal Bureau of Reclamation delivered irrigation water from a tributary of the Colorado River to Utah farmers. This transfer of water was highly subsidized by the federal treasury. The price to the farmers was only $8 per acre-foot (enough water to cover an acre 1-foot deep) even though the cost of the delivered water was about $400 per acre-foot. Estimates put the value of the water to farmers at about $30 per acre-foot.[5]

The below-cost water delivery served the landowners and farmers and the small communities where they live. The high costs (above the amounts the farmers paid) were passed on to taxpayers across the nation. Because each individual taxpayer only paid a fraction of the total cost, to this day most taxpayers have never heard of the project and have no idea of the costs they paid.

Environmental regulations also are frequently influenced by groups such as business firms and unions seeking protection from competitors in the marketplace. The Clean Air Act Amendments of 1977 are a classic illustration of how factional political interests can override the public interest.[6]

These amendments required coal-burning electric power plants to install expensive scrubbing devices in their smokestacks to reduce sulfur dioxide emissions. However, in many cases, the emissions of

---

[5] These figures are from Terry L. Anderson and Pamela S. Snyder, *Priming the Invisible Pump* (Bozeman, Mont.: PERC, 1997), 10.

[6] See Bruce A. Ackerman and William T. Hassler, *Clean Coal/Dirty Air or How the Clean Air Act Became a Multibillion Bail-Out for High-Sulfur Coal Producers and What Should Be Done About It* (New Haven: Yale University Press, 1981); and Robert W. Crandall, "Economic Rents as a Barrier to Deregulation," The *Cato Journal* 6, no. 1 (Spring/Summer 1986), 186–189.

sulfur dioxide could have been reduced merely by using cheap, low-sulfur coal. Because coal companies and their unions in places such as West Virginia and Kentucky produce high-sulfur coal, they didn't want competition from low-sulfur coal, most of which comes from the West. So, working through their political representatives, they froze out the competition by insisting on scrubbers, which won't even work when used with low-sulfur coal. Most voters didn't realize that they would pay more for electric power because of these regulations and that their air would be a little dirtier.

A number of factors combine to make special interest groups far more powerful in a representative democracy than their numbers would indicate.[7] Members of an interest group—such as the owners of specific tracts of farmland irrigated with low-cost water—have a strong stake in the outcome of some political decisions. Thus they have an incentive to hire lobbyists to help them in Congress and regulatory agencies. They also have an incentive to inform themselves and their allies in local communities and to let legislators know how strongly they feel about an issue of special importance. Many of them will vote for or against candidates for election strictly on the basis of whether they support their specific interests. Such interest groups are also in a position to provide financial campaign contributions to candidates who support their positions.

In contrast, most other voters know little about someone else's special-interest issue. For the nonspecial-interest voter, examining the issue takes much more time and energy than it is worth in terms of possible personal gain from eliminating the subsidy or other special help. Of course, there are many such issues, but each would have to be considered separately, so most nonspecial-interest voters simply ignore such issues.

If you were a vote-seeking politician, what would you do? Clearly, on a specific issue in which a special interest is taking a position without organized opposition, there is little to be gained from supporting the interest of the majority, which is largely uninformed and therefore uninterested. Supporting the position of the well-organized group can generate vocal supporters, campaign workers, and importantly, campaign contributions.

---

[7]The following section is adapted from Chapter 3 of James D. Gwartney and Richard L. Stroup, *Economics: Private and Public Choice* (Fort Worth: Dryden Press, 1997).

The ability of the voter to punish politicians for supporting costly special-interest legislation is further hindered by the fact that many issues are bundled together when the voter chooses between one candidate and another. Even if the voter knows and dislikes the politician's stand on one or a few issues, the bundling of hundreds of future issues into one choice between candidates will severely limit the voter's ability to take a stand at the ballot box for or against any particular issue.

Officials of government agencies—bureaucrats—also favor many special-interest programs. The bureaucrats who staff an agency usually want to see their department's goals furthered, whether the goals are to protect more wilderness, build more roads, or provide additional subsidized irrigation projects. To accomplish these goals requires larger budgets and staffs. Not so incidentally, the programs provide the bureaucrats with expanded career opportunities while helping to satisfy their professional aspirations as well. Bureaus, therefore, are usually happy to work to expand their programs to deliver benefits to special-interest groups who, in turn, work with politicians to expand their bureau budgets and programs.

7. Government policies that erode the protection of property rights reduce the ability and the incentive of owners to protect and conserve their resources.

Many environmental policies erode property rights. When they do, they often work against the very environmental protection they are intended to protect. The unintended results can sometimes be dramatic.

The Endangered Species Act, intended to save species thought to be in danger of extinction, is an example.[8] Only 13 of the approximately 1,800 listed species have recovered since the act was passed in 1973. This act is not a success story by any measure. The far-reaching powers vested in federal agents to control the landowners' use of their properties have sometimes worked to protect endangered species, but often have had the opposite effect.

The landowner who provides a good habitat for a listed species, even by accident, is likely to suffer a loss of the right to use the land.

[8]This discussion is based on Richard L. Stroup, *The Endangered Species Act: Making Innocent Species the Enemy*, PERC Policy Series PS-3 (Bozeman, Mont.: PERC, April 1995).

Michael Bean, an environmental defense attorney who is sometimes informally credited with authorship of the Endangered Species Act, explained this to a group that included Fish and Wildlife Service officials. He said that there is "increasing evidence that at least some private landowners are actively managing their lands so as to avoid potential endangered species problems." He emphasized that these actions are "not the result of malice toward the environment" but "fairly rational decisions, motivated by a desire to avoid potentially significant economic constraints." He called them a "predictable response to the familiar perverse incentives that sometimes accompany regulatory programs, not just the endangered species program but others."[9]

The case of Benjamin Cone Jr. is a cautionary tale.[10] Cone inherited 7,200 acres of land in Pender County, North Carolina. He has managed the land primarily for wildlife. He has planted chuffa and rye for wild turkey, for example, and the wild turkey has made a comeback in Pender County partly due to his efforts. He has also frequently conducted controlled burns of the property to improve the habitat for quail and deer.

Red-cockaded woodpeckers are listed as an endangered species. They nest in the cavities of old trees and are attracted to places that have both old trees and a clear understory. By clearing the understory to protect quail and deer and by selectively cutting small amounts of timber, Cone may have helped attract the woodpecker. Cone knew that he had at least a couple of red-cockaded woodpeckers on the property.

When Cone intended to sell some timber from his land, the presence of the birds was formally recorded by the U.S. Fish and Wildlife Service. The agency warned Cone not to cut trees or take any other actions that might disturb the birds. They did not, however, tell Cone where the nests were. Cone hired a wildlife biologist, who estimated that there were 29 birds in 12 colonies. According to the FWS guidelines then in effect for the red-cockaded woodpecker, a circle with a half-mile radius had to be drawn around each colony,

[9]From the transcript of a talk by Michael Bean at a U.S. Fish and Wildlife Service seminar November 3, 1994, Marymount University, Arlington, Va.

[10]Lee Ann Welch, *Property Rights Conflicts under the Endangered Species Act: Protection of the Red-Cockaded Woodpecker*, PERC Working Paper No. 94–12 (Bozeman, Mont.: PERC, 1994).

within which no timber could be harvested. If Cone harvested the timber, he would be subject to a severe fine, possible imprisonment, or both under the ESA.

Biologists estimated that the presence of the birds and the FWS rules put 1,560 acres of Cone's land under the restrictions of the Fish and Wildlife Service.

In response, Cone changed his management techniques. He began to clear-cut 300 to 500 acres every year on the rest of his land. He told an investigator, "I cannot afford to let those woodpeckers take over the rest of the property. I'm going to start massive clear-cutting. I'm going to a 40-year rotation instead of a 75- to 80-year rotation."[11] By harvesting younger trees, Cone could keep the woodpecker from making new nests in old tree cavities. He also took steps to challenge the FWS in court, asking to be compensated for his losses. The agency, however, avoided that court challenge by negotiating a settlement that gave Cone more freedom to use his land.

Cone's experience teaches a lesson to all landowners who learn about his situation. They may be in for similar treatment unless they do something about it. Indeed, after Cone informed the firm's owner of the neighboring land about possible liabilities in connection with the red-cockaded woodpecker, he noticed that the owner clear-cut the property.[12] Overall, what has been the result of the ESA for the red-cockaded woodpecker? As Bean has said, "The red-cockaded woodpecker is closer to extinction today than it was a quarter century ago when the protection began." Bean recommends that the rules be changed to help landowners avoid large reductions in the value of their land from the application of the ESA, but no change in the law is currently in sight.

By using the ESA to justify land use controls that seriously erode the property rights of land owners, the Fish and Wildlife Service has ignored the important positive role that private landowners and institutions have historically played in protecting rare fauna and flora. As mentioned previously, the Delta Waterfowl Foundation has a low-cost adopt-a-pothole program. It pays small amounts to farmers who protect prairie potholes, which are depressions in the land that harbor nesting areas for ducks. What would happen if the

[11] Ike C. Sugg, "Ecosystem Babbitt-Babble," *The Wall Street Journal*, April 2, 1993, A12.
[12] Welch op cit., 47.

ducks became listed species? It seems safe to say that farmers who now cooperate for little or nothing to help the ducks would be wary of enticing listed species onto their lands, even for large payments. Why should an owner risk the loss of control on much of the farm?

8. When the government promotes the goals of some citizens at the expense of others, resources are diverted from production into political action.

As we have seen, the government sometimes forces the transfer of resources from some groups to others without compensating the losers. Interest groups have learned that they can benefit by influencing these transfers. This gradually causes a shift in the economy. Hiring lobbyists to influence laws and tax experts to find loopholes becomes more important relative to hiring innovative scientists, engineers, and production personnel. The output-expanding, positive-sum activities of market discovery, innovation, and production are increasingly replaced by resource-consuming, negative-sum battles to gain political transfers or avoid paying for transfers to others.

As transfers that depend on political clout increase, more people redirect their energies to gaining political influence, taking away more time, energy, and other resources from productive activities. Competition shifts from innovations in production and trade to competing for political favors. When political redistribution of society's goods and services (the pie) grows, fighting over shares reduces efforts devoted to increasing the size of the pie, making it smaller. As the political stakes have grown, we can see the increasing diversion of resources toward use in lobbying activities. The U.S. Senate reported 3,403 individuals registered to lobby in the Senate in 1977. By 1995 the number had grown to 51,381. Environmental regulation no doubt was part of the reason for this increase. The cost of environmental regulation grew rapidly during the same period, rising from $51 billion in 1977 to $218 billion in 2000.[13]

The stated purpose of regulation is seldom to transfer wealth from one group to another. But regulation almost always does just that.

---

[13] Wayne Crews Jr., *Ten Thousand Commandments: A Policymaker's Snapshot of the Federal Regulatory State (2000 Edition)* (Washington, D.C.: Competitive Enterprise Institute, 1998), citing cost estimates from 1977 to 2000 by Thomas Hopkins, compiled for the U.S. Small Business Administration, 4.

We saw earlier in this chapter that stiff environmental regulations for new plants helped regions with high-sulfur coal keep out competition from the low-sulfur coal mines, primarily in the West. Similarly, in the late 1980s there was litigation to strictly enforce existing regulations to prevent used motor oil from being cheaply incinerated in cement kilns. The result would have helped a coalition of waste treatment companies to get more used-oil disposal business. The waste treatment companies joined environmental activist groups to support the legislation.

By forcing some firms to bear greater regulatory burdens, environmental regulation often helps the competitors of those firms.[14]

Efficient use of resources is not the only victim of increased transfer activities. Government is respected when it enhances economic growth and otherwise improves the welfare of citizens. But the legitimacy of government may suffer when it increasingly taxes some citizens to provide transfer payments to others, or when it transfers the use of government lands from groups that have less political influence at the time, giving land use over to other more politically favored groups. Those who lose income or lose access to resources without compensation are often upset. For them and for others who do not benefit from the transfers, these transfer programs make the public-interest rhetoric of government action seem hollow. Political battles over economic benefits for one group at the expense of others create ill will, and that in itself can harm the public welfare.

9. The government's environmental monitoring services can help provide information about the environment that property rights and markets might not produce.

In spite of heavy intervention in the realm of environmental regulation, the federal government has done little in an area where its contribution could be critical—the collection and preservation of data. Whatever system is responsible for controlling pollution—whether property rights and common law or government regulation—good data are needed. It is necessary to know where pollutants are causing harm and where the pollutants are coming from and whether pollution levels are improving or becoming worse.

[14]See, for example, Bruce Yandle, *Common Sense and Common Law for the Environment* (Lanham, Md.: Rowman & Littlefield, 1997), 63–85.

Government-maintained monitoring systems, such as a network of sensing equipment that records the level of pollution at many locations, can provide geographically detailed information that can help explain whether changes resulted from the addition or subtraction of effluents from specific sources, from new industry mixes, or from other origins. Such information can help epidemiological researchers trying to learn when pollutant exposure at various levels is correlated with harms to people and property, and when it is not. They may observe what they think are the effects of pollutants, but if they do not know how high the levels of pollution are, they will have trouble connecting pollution levels with harmful effects.

The federal government has received much criticism for not doing enough to learn about actual pollution levels. Debra Knopman, an environmental scientist and former U.S. Interior Department official in the Clinton administration, put it this way:

> Imagine controlling the heat and air conditioning in a 50-room mansion with one cheap thermostat, or pulling smoke detectors off the mansion walls to save on buying batteries. Compared to the cost of wasted electricity or damage from fire, such penny pinching on monitoring temperature and smoke in the mansion is simply absurd. Yet, this is precisely what we do when we regulate the environment while so poorly monitoring our progress or keeping tabs on how conditions in the air, water and land are changing over time.[15]

Among the examples Knopman notes is a sparse and underfunded water quality monitoring network; it can barely tell us anything about progress under the Clean Water Act. Nor does a national monitoring network exist to measure small particulate matter in the air, for which the Environmental Protection Agency recently issued a stringent new standard.

Regulators need these data to make rational decisions. The common-law protection of property rights against harmful pollution would also be well served with such data. Individuals who fear harm and those who are accused of harmful pollution who contend

---

[15]Debra S. Knopman, "Pennywise, Billions Foolish: The Folly of Underinvestment in Environmental Monitoring" at www.speakout.com/activism/opinions/3437-1.html. Cited June 17, 2002.

they are innocent would value this information. Expanding government data-gathering of ambient pollution levels would seem to be quite useful, especially since regulators are in fact making decisions that could benefit greatly from the information not currently being gathered. But because government decisionmakers do not face the consequences of their poorly informed decisions, they have little incentive to ensure that accurate information is obtained.

10. Competition is important in governmental processes, just as it is in markets.

When state parks were forced to compete for consumer support by becoming reliant on user fees, they found ways to enhance the services they provided. The same could be done for the U.S. Forest Service. For years, environmentalists have complained that the Forest Service is excessively influenced by the timber industry. Instead of using its budget to provide trails and campsites to serve the growing number of people hiking and camping in the national forests, the Forest Service emphasized logging. Randal O'Toole, an environmentalist and forest economist, argued that the solution to this problem was competition. The Forest Service should start charging fees to people hiking in the woods. Those fees, he said, would give Forest Service officials an incentive to do more for hikers and backpackers, including perhaps avoiding some of the clear-cuts they objected to. Some of this change has come about. As part of the federal fee demonstration program that raises or introduces fees in four government agencies, the Forest Service is earning funds. Some funds are going into rehabilitating trails and providing camper services. In essence, competition from recreation is changing the budgetary allocations.

Competition, whether it affects government agencies or private firms, is a disciplinary force. Competition protects consumers against high prices, shoddy merchandise, or poor service. When customers have choices, poor goods and services cause providers to lose business to rivals offering a better deal. We all recognize this point in the private sector. Competition in the public sector can be equally important in helping to provide constructive incentives for agency and program managers.

The incentive structures facing most government agencies and enterprises do not reward officials for efficient operation. The directors and managers of public-sector enterprises can seldom gain by working to reduce cost and improve performance. In fact, if an agency finds and uses cost-cutting measures and thus fails to spend all of this year's budget allocation, it has a weaker case for keeping or enlarging its budget for next year. Agencies typically spend all of each year's appropriation, even if it means spending a lot on low-priority items late in the budget period.

In the private sector, the profit rate is a measure of how much value was added relative to the purchase cost of resources used. Profit provides a clear index of performance. In a competitive market, when property rights are protected, a high profit indicates that resources were purchased at a price lower than the resulting product was worth to buyers. A loss indicates that the product was worth less than the resources taken from the rest of the economy to produce it. In the private sector, low-profit rates or bankruptcy eventually weed out inefficiency.

But there is no indicator of performance such as profit in the public sector, so managers of government firms can often continue despite economic inefficiency. There is no mechanism in the public sector that parallels private-sector bankruptcy or withdrawal due to low profits to end wasteful programs. In fact, poor performance and failure to achieve objectives are often used as arguments for increased funding in the public sector. As the Washington Monument strategy illustrated, National Park Service administrators use poor service to visitors (or the threat of poor service) to argue for increased funding. Every agency uses some form of this method simply to protect and enhance its budget.

Given the incentive structure within the public sector, it is vitally important that government units face competitors. The competition will improve performance, reduce costs, and stimulate innovative behavior. As a result, the waste of resources can be reduced and citizens will get more for their money.

One way that competition is introduced in government is to force agencies to seek part or all of their budgets from user fees. Another way is to decentralize decisionmaking. Citizens can vote with their feet. States and municipalities vary in the degree to which they accept the burdens of environmental regulation to gain the benefits, and tax themselves for the provision of government services. Just as people differ on how much they want to spend for housing or automobiles, so too they will have different views on how much to sacrifice for specific environmental benefits. Some will prefer a high level of environmental services and be willing to pay higher taxes for them. Others will prefer lower tax and regulatory burdens and fewer environmental benefits. A decentralized system can accommodate these divergent views.

Decentralization also allows for competition among local governments, thus helping to promote governmental innovation and efficiency. When citizens can easily vote with their feet, the incentive of government to provide services economically is enhanced. If a government regulates in a costly way (when lower cost methods are available) or levies high taxes without providing a parallel value to voters, both individuals and businesses will be repelled. Similarly, when people bear burdens for items that provide them with little or no value, many will choose the exit option. Thus, like business firms in the marketplace, local governments that fail to serve their citizens will lose customers—that is, population—and tax revenues.

Competition among decentralized governments serves the interests of the citizen. If competition is going to work, however, the policies of the federal government must not stifle it. When a central government subsidizes, mandates, and regulates the bundle of government services provided by local governments, it undermines the competitive process among them.

Conclusion

We cannot expect government managers, if given the authority, simply to fix the shortcomings of the court-enforced property rights and market trading system. They may be able to make some contribution, but they experience incentives and information problems that lead to unintended consequences.

When the government uses its power to increasingly tax, spend, and regulate, more groups try to turn that power to their own narrow advantage. For most citizens, the results do not necessarily improve their situations before government management, and may instead worsen them.

Yet the fact remains that for a few kinds of problems, such as smog in the Los Angeles basin, enforcing property rights does not appear to be a feasible way to protect human health and other values, at least for now. When private enforcement is not available, coercive mechanisms may be the only alternative, for better or for worse. What criteria can help us to choose wisely between private and political management of the environment? Chapter 4 examines that question.

4. Choosing: Economics and Environmental Policy Choices

Two different types of economic systems can be used to address environmental problems. One system emphasizes politics and government organization. The other system relies primarily on private property rights and market relationships. Each uses different signals to communicate what people want. And each provides different incentives that lead individuals to heed those signals.

This chapter further explores both the market mechanism and the direct government controls, with the goal of evaluating the role of each. It begins with the market approach, which was used initially in the United States to deal with most environmental problems. More recently, the market approach has been supplemented and even supplanted by the political approach.

Addressing environmental problems through markets occurs through the exchange of property rights (buying and selling property) and reliance on common-law courts and law officers. Since the government provides the courts and law officers, the market approach also involves some political decisions because people vote for the judges or for the politicians who will appoint the judges. However, with he market approach the government is in the background. The actual environmental results are largely determined by a combination of the evolving technologies and the evolving preferences of those who participate in the market and bear the consequences of their actions. This arrangement can limit harmful pollution, encourage conservation, and thus protect and enhance the environment.

In the past, the private rights and market option served as environmental policy in the United States and parts of Europe. Although these nations experienced periods of pollution and some harm to the environment, the market allowed for improvements in health, longevity, and other quality-of-life characteristics over several centuries. It also led to the control of severe pollution, the restoration of harmed areas, and the protection of large areas of land.

Efforts to preserve, enhance, and restore the environment increased as people in these countries became more affluent. Real estate developers paid more attention to preserving green space—and sometimes even habitat for wildlife—within residential areas, both in metropolitan areas and in the resorts where people vacationed. Private organizations such as the Nature Conservancy and the Delta Waterfowl Foundation developed ways to protect endangered species and to preserve large tracts of land. Private companies like Prairie Restorations, Inc., responded to the desire of many people to live around more natural or indigenous plants and flowers, while other innovators developed ecotourism—travel that showcases and protects natural environmental treasures such as the rain forests and wildlife. Adaptation and innovation are constant processes in a market system, and the growing interest in nature spurred new ways to support environmental protection.

The market approach was too weak to serve some of the environmental goals that many people wanted. It relied on the courts to protect individual rights against polluters or others who would misuse resources, and the courts did not always respond effectively. The system has never satisfactorily reduced certain kinds of air pollution in big cities such as Los Angeles or London, for example, where a great many polluters simultaneously harm a great many citizens. Economic incentives to save fuel and avoid lawsuits helped, but serious pollution problems remained. As a result of these shortcomings, and for other reasons as well, direct government control has increasingly replaced the market system over the past three decades.

Direct governmental control of the environment operates through two means. One is through regulating of individual behavior by government agencies such as the Environmental Protection Agency. The other is through government ownership and management of resources, primarily land and water. The two may be combined, for example, when residents of a city are taxed to pay for a government-owned sewage treatment plant. In this case, the government requires citizens to contribute to the cleanup of waste and it also owns the mechanism used for that cleanup. Either way, this approach is generally called command-and-control environmental policy.

Since 1970, command-and-control has become the most frequently chosen type of environmental policy. In place of individual decisions and market trading, elected officials and agency appointees decide on the goals and often specify the means used to seek environmental protection. Each system has strengths and weaknesses.

Each modern industrial nation relies on a mix of the two approaches. As policymakers consider the future, they may have opportunities to change the mix. How much should we rely on property rights and market trading for environmental policy, and when should we turn to command-and-control instead? And can they work together? To answer these questions, here are 10 key points to consider.

1. Producing and protecting environmental quality are similar to producing and protecting any other good or service; individuals must receive accurate signals about what others want from them, and each must have incentives to heed those signals.

Many people think of the environment as different, yet producing and protecting environmental quality are similar to producing and protecting any other good or service. A forest, for example, can supply many goods and services. These can include logs for houses and pulp for paper. A forest can also include streams for recreation and habitat for wildlife. Some of these goods—logs and, frequently, access to wildlife for hunting, fishing, and camping—are traditionally sold on the market. Others, like habitat for wild animals, are less often bought and sold for that purpose. Whatever economic system we choose to address environmental decisions must coordinate the desires of people who control the resources—whether government managers or private owners—with the desires of those who want to use them. Getting people to do what is needed for the good of others, and getting them to refrain from wasteful or harmful acts requires the right informational signals and the right incentives. And in the case of direct governmental control, where neither market prices nor the profit motive guides users and producers, the means to force compliance with political decisions must be implemented.

2. Economic institutions matter. Economies around the world grow more rapidly and produce more goods and services per person, including environmental quality, when the role of government is smaller.

The productivity and wealth of nations depend as much on their institutions—the laws, incentives, and rules in place—as on their

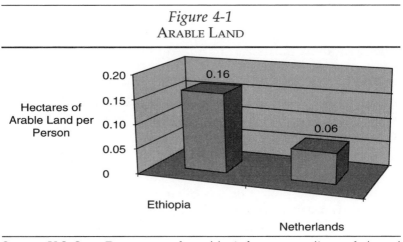

Figure 4-1
ARABLE LAND

Hectares of Arable Land per Person

SOURCE: U.S. State Department, http://usinfo.state.gov/journals/otes/0502/ijee/arable.htm.

natural resources. Whether property rights can be traded, and under what conditions, can be more important than land or other physical aspects of a nation in determining how well people live.

Some people question this claim. They tend to think that if a country has good arable soil, it will produce adequate crops, or if it has plenty of rivers and ports, it will engage in trade. Through these natural resources, wealth will develop naturally. One very simple comparison will challenge that assumption.

Figure 4-1 shows that Ethiopia has about three times as much good farmland per person as the Netherlands. Good farmland has fertile soil, good weather, and enough rainfall to support substantial crop production. Yet in the mid-1990s, Ethiopia was barely able to produce enough food to feed itself.

Figure 4-2 shows that in 2001 Ethiopia exported, on net, only $4.02 per person worth of agricultural products. Ethiopia is a socialist nation that did not allow property rights to be protected and freely traded. It was also engaged in frequent wars with neighbors. In contrast, the Netherlands exported $904 per person worth of agricultural products that year, even though it had only about a third as much good farmland per person. The Netherlands relies primarily on markets and trade to spur agricultural production. Although a number of factors may influence the productivity of Ethiopia and

Figure 4-2
NET AGRICULTURAL EXPORTS PER CAPITA IN 2001

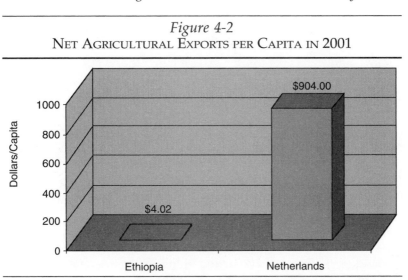

SOURCE: Food and Agricultural Organization of the United States. FAO Statistical Database, http://apps.fao.org/default.htm. Accessed June 8, 2002.

the Netherlands, the message that institutions can matter a great deal in producing agricultural output—more than the available land in some situations—comes across loud and clear.

One comparison of this sort can be a good illustration, but it proves nothing. Even dozens of comparisons, randomly chosen, might not be persuasive, since most nations are not as easily classified into "market-oriented" or "nonmarket" nations as are the Netherlands and Ethiopia.

To compare the results of the market approach with the results of command-and-control more systematically, we need to know the extent to which markets and government control are used in each nation studied and then to compare characteristics of those nations. Economists James Gwartney of Florida State University and Robert Lawson of Capital University, using their own research together with that of many others over an eight-year period, enable us to do this. They have constructed an index measuring the degree to which private decisions and voluntary exchange drive the economy of each nation.[1] The summary rating is called an economic freedom index.

[1]James Gwartney and Robert Lawson, *Economic Freedom of the World Annual Report 2001* (Vancouver, B.C.: The Fraser Institute, 2001).

The higher scores reflect a greater role for private owners and a greater freedom to own property, to receive protection for it under the law, and to be able to freely trade with others. The lower scores represent a greater degree of government decisionmaking in the economy.

The scores calculated by Gwartney and Lawson for 123 nations in 1999 range from 1.9 to 9.4. Countries having the smallest role for private property rights and voluntary exchange—the least amount of economic freedom by this measure—have the lowest scores. In 1999 these included Myanmar (1.9), Algeria (2.6), Democratic Republic of Congo (3.0), Guinea-Bissau (3.3), and Sierra Leone (3.5). At the other end of the spectrum are the countries that have the most respect for private property rights and voluntary exchange. In 1999, these were the United States (8.7), the United Kingdom (8.8), New Zealand (8.9), Singapore (9.3), and Hong Kong (9.4). (Note that the economic system and economic freedom, rather than the political system and political freedom, are measured in this rating system.)

One way to use this index is to see how economic freedom or government control correlates with attributes such as a nation's worker productivity or agricultural output. When the 123 nations are ranked by economic freedom (with the top 20 percent or top quintile in one group, the next 20 percent into another group, and so on, down to the lowest 20 percent or lowest quintile), we find many favorable factors associated with more market influence and less government control over the economy.

For example, Figure 4-3 shows that more economic freedom is associated with greater productivity of cereal grains per acre of good farmland. In other words, when government decisions play a larger role in a nation's economy, relative to market decisions, a key indicator of agricultural productivity—cereal grain production per acre—goes down.

The implications of the economic freedom index are extremely broad. They go far beyond cereal grain production. Figures 4-4 and 4-5, directly from the work of Gwartney and Lawson, show that economies with a greater role for private ownership and market decisions tend to exhibit both greater prosperity and more rapid economic growth. In other words, economies that are oriented toward free markets have performed better economically than those with more government decisionmaking.

Figure 4-3
CEREAL CROP YIELDS RISE WITH ECONOMIC FREEDOM

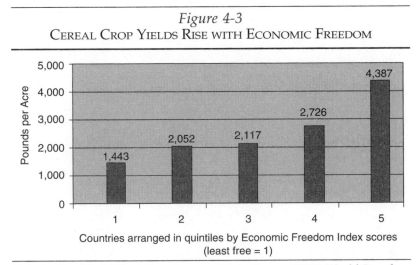

SOURCE: The World Bank Development Data Group. "2001 World Development Indicators."

Figure 4-4
ECONOMIC FREEDOM AND PROSPERITY

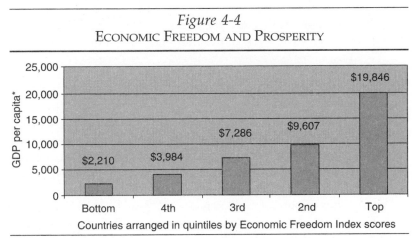

SOURCE: Gwartney and Lawson, *Economic Freedom of the World Annual Report 2001*, p. 11. In 1998 international dollars, adjusted for purchasing power parity (PPP).

For citizens in nations with higher income growth rates and higher income levels, even the poor can live well. For example, in the United

Figure 4-5
ECONOMIC FREEDOM AND GROWTH

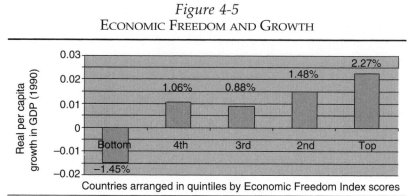

Countries arranged in quintiles by Economic Freedom Index scores

SOURCE: Gwartney and Lawson, *Economic Freedom of the World Annual Report 2001*, p. 11.

States, the income that is officially considered poverty level is more than twice the median income per person for the world.[2] In the United States, 72 percent of poverty-income households have a washing machine and the same number have one or more cars. Ninety-three percent have a color TV and 98 percent have a refrigerator.[3] The main point is this: Economic institutions affect what people do and how they live, even more than natural resources do.

3. Political and bureaucratic institutions tend to reduce efficiency and increase waste; the resulting decisions are less environmentally sound.

A dramatic illustration of what happens when ownership of land and its products are taken from private owners and given to the government followed the Russian revolution of 1917. During the 1920s and 1930s, agricultural land was collectivized—seized by the government. Instead of working their own lands, farmers were assigned to work on giant collectives.

Before the revolution, Russia was known as the breadbasket of the world, producing more grain than any other country. But after the new policy was instituted, grain production fell sharply. Between

[2]Based on national income median figures, weighted by population.

[3]W. Michael Cox and Richard Alm, *Myths of Rich and Poor: Why We're Better Off Than We Think* (New York: Basic Books, 1999), 15.

5 and 10 million Russians starved to death, despite donations of food from nations with market economies.

Because of widespread starvation, the government eventually allowed farm families each to have small private plots of less than one acre, which they could farm for their own use or to sell the produce in local markets. From these tiny privately owned plots, which added up to only 3 percent of the country's crop land, came 27 percent of the nation's food.[4] The Russian farmers, like other resource owners, were more willing to work hard and make productive use of a resource over which they had clear control.

After 1989, when the socialist nations began opening their borders and permitting more movement of goods and people across their borders, the income differences were obvious. So, too, were the differences in the environment. Newspapers and magazines began reporting shocking examples, from drinking water seriously contaminated with arsenic in Hungary to pollution of irrigation water by heavy metals in Bulgaria. A giant pollution zone stretches out into the formerly pristine Lake Baikal, and the Aral Sea has drastically diminished in size due to irrigation for cotton plantations.[5]

The same lack of privately enforceable rights against harms, invasions, and takings—the lack of private property rights—that led to lower incomes and slower growth also led to far greater environmental pollution. Mark Hertsgaard, a writer who journeyed in China in the 1990s, describes visiting a paper mill in Chonqing. He saw a "vast torrent of white, easily 30 yards wide, splashing down the hillside from the rear of the factory like a waterfall of boiling milk."[6] Suddenly, a gas explosion sent him running. This was a factory that was supposed to have been closed down because of excessive pollution. Hertsgaard also reported on the oppressive smoke in China's major cities.

The socialist countries wasted resources. Studies by Mikhail Bernstam of the Hoover Institution found that market-based economies in western Europe used far less energy per $1,000 worth of output

[4]David Osterfeld, *Prosperity versus Planning* (New York: Oxford University Press, 1992), 82.

[5]These examples come from Peter J. Hill, "Environmental Problems Under Socialism," *The Cato Journal* 12, no. 2 (Fall 1992), 321–335. Other examples abound.

[6]Mark Hertsgaard, *Earth Odyssey: Around the World in Search of Our Environmental Future* (New York: Broadway Books, 1999), 3.

than the socialist nations of eastern Europe in 1986. Similarly, the European socialist economies used far more steel per unit of output than the European market economies did.[7]

The bottom line is this: Control of resources by politics and bureaucracies does not bring the same pressures and personal incentives to innovate, to conserve resources, and to avoid damage downwind and downstream that private ownership and market decisions do. Political and bureaucratic decisions tend to be less efficient, more wasteful, and thus less environmentally friendly.

4. Protection of private property rights is associated with healthier environmental conditions and longer lives.

Recent studies show that in countries where property rights are better protected, people are healthier and live longer due to better environmental conditions. For example, using the economic freedom index discussed earlier, Seth Norton found that in countries where property rights are protected, 93 percent of the population have access to safe drinking water, while in nations with weak property rights, only 60 percent of the population have that access. Similarly, in nations with stronger property rights, 93 percent have access to sewage treatment, while only 48 percent do in countries with weak rights.[8] Life expectancy is 70 years in a nation with strong protection of property rights, while it is only 50 years in nations without that level of protection.

One reason for these differences is that economically free nations are generally wealthier, as indicated previously. Certainly, wealthier nations have the wherewithal to take action that protects health, safety, and environmental conditions. Once people satisfy their basic needs, such as providing food on the table, they begin to improve their environmental conditions.

There is more to it than that, however. Norton also conducted a study looking solely at poor nations (countries with per capita

[7]Mikhail S. Bernstam, *The Wealth of Nations and the Environment* (London: Institute of Economic Affairs, 1991), 23–25.

[8]Seth W. Norton, "Property Rights, The Environment, and Economic Well-Being," in *Who Owns the Environment?* Peter J. Hill and Roger E. Meiners, eds. (Lanham, Md.: Rowman & Littlefield, 1998), 37–54.

income less than \$5,000 in 1985).[9] He found that even among poor nations, 95 percent of the population live to age 40 in countries that offer relatively stronger property rights protection, while in the nations with weaker rights protection, only 74 percent of the people live to age 40. In rich nations or poor, property rights make an important difference. When it comes to basic environmental protection—such as protecting water supplies and providing access to clean water—a system that protects private property rights is superior to one that relies on direct government control. Ownership of the land or other asset gives the owner a legal right to use the courts to protect it. The owner has both the right and the incentive to protect, and to find highly valued uses for, the owned asset.

5. Replacing property rights (protected by the common law) with politically determined protection levels can result in lower environmental standards.

As noted earlier, the courts in a market economy are sometimes unable to protect rights against pollution. For example, if individuals cannot persuasively show the court that they are being harmed by pollution, the court will not stop polluters or make them pay damages. Failure by the courts to protect property rights can prevent the proper flow of incentives in the same way that failure to enforce laws and regulations of any sort can defeat the intent of the law.

That fact does not mean that government control will perform better.[10] One of the events that launched the modern environmental movement was the report in 1969 that the Cuyahoga River, which goes through the city of Cleveland and empties into Lake Erie, was so polluted that it burned. Of course, the water didn't literally burn, but there was oil on the water and lots of debris; a spark, probably from a train, ignited it. Public outrage at the thought that a river could go up in flames galvanized action and helped bring about tougher laws.[11]

---

[9] Seth W. Norton, "Poverty, Property Rights, and Human Well-Being: A Cross-National Study," *The Cato Journal* 18, no. 2 (Fall 1998), 233–245.

[10] See Neil K. Komesar, *Imperfect Alternatives* (Chicago: University of Chicago Press, 1994), Chapters 1 and 2, for a full explanation of the nature of this institutional choice question.

[11] Roger E. Meiners, Stacie Thomas, and Bruce Yandle, "Burning Rivers, Common Law, and Institutional Choice for Water Quality," in *The Common Law and the Environment*, Roger E. Meiners and Andrew P. Morriss, eds. (Lanham, Md.: Rowman & Littlefield, 2000), 54–85.

It turns out that the Cuyahoga fire, which is still famous in some circles, occurred because efforts to obtain relief from river pollution through the courts had been replaced by command-and-control. A state pollution control board was in charge of issuing permits to emit pollutants into the water. The board had decided that a key stretch of the Cuyahoga was an industrial river, so the companies along its banks did not have to clean up their effluent to any significant degree. In 1965, Bar Realty Corporation, a real estate company, had tried to clean up a Cuyahoga tributary, but the Ohio Supreme Court concluded that the state pollution control board, not the courts deciding common-law claims, had the authority—and this board did not require cleanup.

Despite its imperfections, the use of property rights, common law, and market relationships have some real advantages. Although judges and juries are not experts, in court they must listen to experts on both sides, each bound by rules of evidence and cross-examined by the other, before rendering a decision. That is far from the case when even those same individuals (judges and jurors) enter an election booth to vote or when they vote as elected representatives. As indicated in Chapter 3, voters are unlikely to be as informed as if they had been present through a trial of the facts, with its burden of proof, rules of evidence, and rights of cross-examination. With the exception of situations in which there are large numbers of polluters and victims, there is no obvious reason to believe that courts are less informed as they decide an issue than voters, or even congressional representatives, are on that same issue.[12]

In fact, evidence from Canada—where, as in the United States, statutory law and government control have been replacing decisions by private owners—suggests that the common-law protections are stronger. Researcher and writer Elizabeth Brubaker reviewed dozens of legal decisions and statutes. As political control supplanted the common law approach to pollution, the protection of victims was weakened. She writes—

> Governments have shown that they are not up to the task
> of preventing resource degradation or pollution; indeed they
> have often actively encouraged it. . . . It is long past time for

[12]Direct government control, as in EPA regulation, for example, can be aided by bureaucratic experts who advise policymakers. But both the experts and their bureaucratic superiors are likely to have tunnel vision.

> resources to be shifted away from governments and back to
> the individuals and communities that have strong interests
> in their preservation. Such a shift can best be accomplished
> by strengthening property rights and by assigning property
> rights to resources now being squandered by governments.[13]

Brubaker's book shows that property rights had been the better
protector of environmental values. Individuals with property rights
against those who might harm them—governments included—will
gain by finding ways to use those rights effectively to protect themselves and their resources.

6. Environmental policies should be fair and cost-effective.

When government decisions are perceived as unfair, serious social
conflicts can result. In the late 1980s and early 1990s, a property
rights movement erupted around the country, composed of voluntary organizations formed by people who believed that environmental regulations were violating their property rights. Landowners—
many of them small property owners who could not build on
wetlands or who could not log their lands because it contained
endangered species—built this movement. In their view, individual
property owners were being forced to bear the full cost of setting
aside their lands to produce a habitat for wildlife and amenity values
that benefited the public generally. They believed that the cost of
such production should be purchased from willing sellers and thus
more fairly distributed among the general public. The owners of the
land, they reasoned, should pay their share, and no more, of the
cost of a habitat or environmental preservation. This property rights
backlash, in turn, caused a reaction among environmental groups,
who viewed the property rights movement as an attack on environmental goals.

The mechanisms for protecting the environment should also be
cost-effective. Why? The willingness of citizens to pay for higher
environmental quality depends on the cost. Inefficient policies are
more costly per unit of result and do not sell as well to voters as
do more efficient policies. And when the costs are concentrated on
a few, more organized opposition to the conservation project is

---

[13]See Elizabeth Brubaker, *Property Rights in Defense of Nature* (Toronto: EarthScan, 1995), 161.

Figure 4-6
MEDIAN COST/LIFE-YEARS EXTENDED

Federal Aviation Administration	$23,000
Consumer Product Safety Commission	$68,000
National Highway Transportation Safety Administration	$78,000
Occupational Safety and Health Administration	$88,000
Environmental Protection Agency	$7,600,000
Overall for regulations	**$730,000**

SOURCE: Tengs et al. "Five Hundred Life-Saving Interventions and Their Cost-Effectiveness," *Risk Analysis* 15, no. 3, (1995) 369–390.

likely. Policies that achieve desired results without demanding huge economic or other sacrifices are an easier sell for those who care strongly about protecting the environment.

7. The change in pollution control policy from a property rights framework to administrative regulation is causing many Americans to die prematurely.

Many current environmental programs, including those designed to further health and safety, are accomplishing little at high cost. Tammy Tengs and colleagues at the Harvard School of Public Health studied 587 regulations and other federal government programs designed to save lives.[14] They found dramatic differences in the costs of saving lives and preventing illness and injury.

Their comparisons were based on the cost of extending one person's life by one year. Figure 4-6 shows some of the results when they compiled their numbers by agency. They estimate that the cost to save one additional life-year was $23,000 for Federal Aviation Administration regulations and $88,000 for Occupational Safety and Health Administration rules to reduce fatal accidents. Neither agency is especially noted for efficiency, but compare the median cost of their regulations to those of the Environmental Protection Agency. The EPA's regulations impose an estimated cost of $7,600,000 for each additional life-year extended!

If the federal government shifted its resources from carrying out the highest-cost regulations to those that are more cost-effective,

[14]Tammy O. Tengs, Miriam Adams, Joseph Pliskin, Dana Fafran, Joanna Siegel, Milton Weinstein, and John Graham, "Five Hundred Life-Saving Interventions and Their Cost-Effectiveness," *Risk Analysis* 15, no. 3 (1995), 369–390.

more lives would be extended for the same total cost. Alternatively, if the most costly regulations were loosened and the least costly were tightened, the same lifesaving effects could be achieved at far lower cost.

Why are such programs and regulations implemented despite their inefficiency? One answer is that regulators are subject to the tunnel vision discussed in Chapter 3. A regulator recognizes the potential benefits from stringent controls on the particular target for which he or she is responsible, but tends to ignore that hitting that target requires sacrifices by others. This tunnel vision means that a regulator often sees the goal as helping people by means of the regulator's specific program rather than helping people by all of the programs put together. Yet for the American people, who are presumably interested in the full complement of programs, excessive zeal for one program reduces the resources available to others and may be counterproductive.

Another reason is selective and misleading communication about risks. George Gray and John Graham of the Harvard Center for Risk Analysis reviewed an EPA report on the risks caused by exposure to toxic air pollutants. They concluded that the EPA "has misled journalists, policymakers, and the American people about what is known about the carcinogenic effects of certain air pollutants."[15] They found that prominent journalists, an important environmental leader, and even William Reilly, the EPA Administrator at that time, had all misinterpreted the report. Their interpretation reflected the report's summary rather than its more careful and accurate main narrative with its supporting data and calculations. The agency's misleading treatment of its own information feeds the fears of citizens and encourages demands for more stringent controls.

Such distortion leads voters to allow—and in some cases demand—regulatory programs that waste resources when other programs could have used those resources to save additional lives. The end result has often been to expend large amounts of resources to achieve small marginal gains in risk reduction, as in the case of Superfund.

[15]George M. Gray and John D. Graham, "Risk Assessment and Clean Air Policy," *Journal of Policy Analysis and Management* 10, no. 2 (1991), 286–295, at 286. They analyzed the 1989 Environmental Protection Agency publication, *Cancer Risk from Outdoor Exposure to Air Toxics.*

One reason why voters tend to ignore the costs of environmental programs is that many mistakenly believe that corporations, not people, are paying the costs of reducing air pollutants or cleaning up chemical wastes. In fact, the cost of such regulations is spread among the firms' customers, employees, and shareholders. Fortunately, as more and more American invest in stock and thus own significant amounts of corporate shares, voters may begin to realize that they are bearing a share of *all* of the costs placed on business.

8. Market-like incentive schemes ("market-based mechanisms") are not the same as markets.

Economists often propose that the government address environmental problems by mimicking the private sector. It is now popular for economics textbooks to discuss pricing and market-like mechanisms for environmental policy, and a few environmental groups have supported limited examples of such mechanisms, including the air emissions trading allowed in the Clean Air Act Amendments of 1990.

These mechanisms became acceptable as environmental goals grew more ambitious and the cost of meeting those goals grew. Because of the high cost, elected officials and other policymakers have begun to recognize how pricing, and even trading rights in an artificial market for pollution permits, could substantially reduce the cost of reaching environmental goals. There are two major approaches:

1. *Pollution charges* are levied by government on a polluter. Ideally, these charges would just equal the costs borne by others downwind or downstream. By facing these costs, the polluter would have an incentive to reduce the emissions in order to reduce the tax. As emissions went down, the payment by the company would go down—to the point at which the cost of more reduction would be larger than the further reduction in emission charges. At that point, the company would pay what remained of the tax. This process would result in efficient emission controls.

Revenue from the charges could, in principle, be given as compensation to those downwind or downstream who actually bear the costs of the remaining pollution. In practice, however, this does not happen with existing pollution charge schemes in the United States. In fact, there are only a few examples of pollution charges of this kind in the United States. This is probably due to lobbying pressure from those who would pay, since the charges are an added cost of doing business. But there is an extra dimension: Governments would not be happy with these charges, either. The more effective companies were in controlling pollution, the less tax revenue there would be.

Emission charges have another problem: they do not allow for the flexibility of trades. Authorities announce the rules of behavior rather than establish tradable rights. Bargaining and trades among emitters and receptors seeking mutual benefits are not allowed.

2. *Trading systems* operate differently. The pollution control authority (such as the Environmental Protection Agency) sets the total amount of emissions allowed in an area. Then it assigns (or perhaps sells) permits allowing emission of that amount of pollution. These permits are tradable.

Tradable permits give emitters an incentive to reduce or even eliminate emissions. If they can reduce emissions cheaply, they may achieve enough reductions so that they can sell their emissions permits to others who face higher costs. In other words, they may not need all their permits, which may be valuable to others. Those who cannot reduce their emissions cheaply may consider buying permits from those who have been able to do so.

Each polluter will reduce pollution up to the point where the added cost of reducing pollution further does not pay for itself. Some polluters (the ones who can reduce pollution cheaply) will reduce it as long as they can offset their costs by selling permits. Other polluters (for whom reduction is more expensive) will reduce emissions to the point where it would be cheaper to pay a more efficient producer to cut back.

Efficiency in the attainment of the emission levels chosen by the pollution control authority should result. To reach the chosen goal, the authority need not know in advance which of the emitters can control more cheaply, nor what technology is best used by the various emitters.

The best-known example is the system of tradable permits to emit sulfur dioxide that was established in the Clean Air Act Amendments of 1990. This act authorized the EPA to establish a nationwide program for trading sulfur-dioxide emission reductions among power plants. This program is lowering the long-run compliance costs of electric utilities meeting legislated targets for those reductions. The utilities that face the highest cost of emission control are purchasing permits from those who can control more of their emissions at lower cost and who thus have permits to sell.

This was not the nation's first pollution credit trading program. During the 1980s, refiners were required to phase out lead in gasoline. Lead had been an important performance-enhancing additive in gasoline. When emitted by automobiles, it dangerously polluted the air. Taking lead out of gasoline meant that refiners had to reformulate their gasoline to get the same advantages without lead. Rather than simply demand that each producer of gasoline take the lead out immediately, permits were distributed on the basis of past production. The EPA allowed low-cost producers of leaded gasoline to purchase production permits from high-cost producers. High-cost producers stopped producing leaded gasoline sooner than a simpler set of command-and-control rules would have dictated. Low-cost producers took up the slack, so the cost of phasing out lead was minimized.

Such schemes can play a useful role, but they come into operation only after an inflexible level of total allowable emissions has been set. Each polluter is assigned rights to emit a certain amount. Then the polluters can trade the rights with one another. All polluters gain from this trading, which should minimize the total costs of the pollution control required to reach the agency-chosen standard.

A major problem for these schemes is the fact that the pollution control authorities need accurate information to set the allowable emissions. What level of emissions would produce a reduction in harm large enough to meet community standards of health and safety? Would a lower level avoid significant property damage to neighbors, or to those downwind or downstream? Would a somewhat higher level of pollution, if allowed, still meet community standards? Without this knowledge, the pollution control authority may worsen the situation rather than improve it—yet this is exactly the same data that the courts need to enforce receptors' rights. When that information is not available, there is no reason to expect government regulation to do better than the courts enforcing common law. And under current U.S. law, regulators usually have no obligation to seek such information.

Regulators have an additional problem that the courts do not. After a court orders a reduction in pollution to meet community standards against harm to others, the polluter and the receptor can then trade property rights if they wish. For example, a court may order a factory owner to reduce a certain pollution flow by half to keep from violating the rights of a downwind farmer. However, the farmer might be willing to accept the pollution without the ordered reduction in exchange for $100,000. If avoiding the extra pollution control would save the polluter $200,000, then at some price in between both would gain. Efficient results would come about, even if the court's order—made without considering the cost of control— was not itself efficient.

With regulation, however, trade cannot usually follow, even though it would benefit all parties. Suppose the Environmental Protection Agency set the same pollution standard as the judge did in the hypothetical case. The farmer downwind might prefer getting $100,000 rather than less pollution, and the factory owner might gladly pay that and more because reducing the pollution would cost more. But the two cannot legally make that trade under an EPA regulation.

Even where trading is allowed, Congress or the EPA could set total allowable emissions so low that no amount of trading could reduce costs enough to make the benefits offset the costs. And the pollution level is not negotiable upward.

Robert Crandall, a Brookings Institution economist, was a self-proclaimed "unabashed advocate of 'market solutions' to environmental problems" when he was a member of the Carter administration in the late 1970s.[16] He championed programs like emissions charges and tradable credits. Today, however, he is more skeptical. "The emissions trading provision," he says, "was buried in a section of the Act that requires an annual 10 million ton rollback of SO_x emissions." This enormous cutback was set even though the problem it was designed to combat—acid rain—had been shown to be "hardly the problem" it had previously been thought to be. "The costs are likely to swamp the benefits," Crandall said about the Clean Air Act Amendments of 1990.

[16]Robert W. Crandall, "Is There Progress in Environmental Policy?" *Contemporary Economic Policy* 12, no. 1 (1994), 80–83.

An efficient way to reach a badly chosen goal may be worse than no action at all. Any hope that incentive-based approaches will improve policy is depends entirely on a proper choice of goals. These problems associated with politically determining the goals may completely overwhelm the benefits that come from market-like mechanisms.

9. Scientists, called upon to evaluate the danger from a particular environmental concern, can be expected to focus attention on the most troublesome future scenarios that they can reasonably project.

Valid information on the science of chemical risks and other environmental harms is not always easy to obtain. Scientists often disagree on the severity of a particular problem, even when they agree on the basic science. For example, there is a lively debate over how serious the threat is of global warming caused by carbon dioxide emitted from the burning of fossil fuels. Issues that spark disagreement include the role of added carbon dioxide on the formation and composition of clouds, the health effects of warmer nights (the main result so far of apparent global warming), and the impact that additional warming might have on the polar ice caps (since they will become smaller in footprint, but may be thicker because of added snowfall).

One thing we can be sure of is that the scientists themselves, especially those in charge of large research projects and laboratories, have an incentive to seek more funding for their programs. Like all of us, they have tunnel vision regarding the importance of their missions. Each believes that his or her mission is exceedingly important relative to other budget priorities.

To obtain more funding, it helps immensely to have the public (and thus Congress and potential private funders) worried about the critical nature of the problem being studied. This incentive makes key researchers unlikely to interpret existing knowledge in a way that reduces public concern. Heightening that concern will help the researcher. Whatever the evidence indicates, such scientists can be expected to emphasize the worst case that can reasonably be projected. "Scientists have realized that frightening the public brings dollars," comments Sylvan Wittwer, a retired biologist from Michigan State University,[17] who has seen environmental crises come and go.

10. Market solutions allow diverse decisions.

No one environmental plan can be best for everyone because, while some goals are shared, the emphasis on each differs among individuals. This idea parallels an important fact in nature: Any change in the environment will help some plants and animals and harm others. So far as is known, nature knows no favorites between one environment and another. Nature does not prefer forests to deserts or wetlands to prairies. Rather, each environment favors some living things over others.

As we seek prosperity, peace in society, and insurance against unforeseen environmental calamities, we should be aware of some major benefits of market solutions to environmental problems.

Market decisions are diverse and decentralized. Many mistakes will be made, but they will have far smaller effects than if central planners made them for the entire society. Those who disagree with a policy, such as the way the Nature Conservancy manages its lands, do not have to support those projects and can therefore be tolerant of others as they implement their preferred options.

Some of the "mistakes," as in the case of Rosalie Edge and her Hawk Mountain Sanctuary discussed earlier, are greatly appreciated later for the benefits they provide. The prosperity that the market system brings about fosters the willingness and the ability to seek and support ever-greater environmental quality.

Conclusion

Although private property rights provide an approach that promotes prosperity and cooperation and at the same time protects the environment, those who want more environmental protection frequently go to the government to obtain it. Government is a powerful tool. That is why it is so important for government to recognize and help to preserve people's rights against theft and the use of force and against invasions such as harmful pollution. Earlier in this chapter, data from around the world showed that such protection

[17]Telephone conversation with Sylvan Wittwer, June 26, 2001.

is vital to a peaceful and successful economy as well as to environmental protection.

Government regulation has had its successes. But we have also observed that government easily goes astray. Government is often used by special interests at the expense of less organized individuals. Protections against the misuse of government consist of—

- The budget process when an agency wants goods and services to further its mission
- The burden of proof and the legal process when an agency exercises police powers to stop wrongful deeds and harmful acts.

If more private-sector control is better, exactly where should government control be shrunk? How should the role of the private sector be expanded? Those questions have been addressed with principles and examples, not with a cookbook of specific recipes. And that is the proper role of economics—helping us to think through each problem more insightfully, so we can apply our own values and beliefs more effectively and better understand the arguments of others. Both the data and the economic principles show clearly that considering markets is a worthwhile endeavor. Although property rights and markets are imperfect, we have seen evidence that they are greatly underappreciated, and thus greatly underused at this point in the history of environmental policy.

Index

About the Author

Richard Stroup is a professor of economics at Montana State University and a senior associate of PERC—the Center for Free Market Environmentalism. Stroup is a widely published author and speaker on economics, including natural resources and environmental issues. His work helped develop the approach to resource problems known initially as the New Resource Economics and now as free-market environmentalism. Stroup is coauthor with James D. Gwartney of a primer on economics, *What Everyone Should Know about Economics and Prosperity*, as well as coauthor with James D. Gwartney, Russell S. Sobel, and David Macpherson of a leading college economics textbook, *Economics: Private and Public Choice*, now in its 10th edition. Stroup received his B.A., M.A., and Ph.D. degrees from the University of Washington. From 1982 to 1984, he was director of the Office of Policy Analysis at the U.S. Department of the Interior. He lives in Bozeman, Montana, with his wife, Jane Shaw Stroup, and his youngest son, David.

Cato Institute

Founded in 1977, the Cato Institute is a public policy research foundation dedicated to broadening the parameters of policy debate to allow consideration of more options that are consistent with the traditional American principles of limited government, individual liberty, and peace. To that end, the Institute strives to achieve greater involvement of the intelligent, concerned lay public in questions of policy and the proper role of government.

The Institute is named for *Cato's Letters*, libertarian pamphlets that were widely read in the American Colonies in the early 18th century and played a major role in laying the philosophical foundation for the American Revolution.

Despite the achievement of the nation's Founders, today virtually no aspect of life is free from government encroachment. A pervasive intolerance for individual rights is shown by government's arbitrary intrusions into private economic transactions and its disregard for civil liberties.

To counter that trend, the Cato Institute undertakes an extensive publications program that addresses the complete spectrum of policy issues. Books, monographs, and shorter studies are commissioned to examine the federal budget, Social Security, regulation, military spending, international trade, and myriad other issues. Major policy conferences are held throughout the year, from which papers are published thrice yearly in the *Cato Journal*. The Institute also publishes the quarterly magazine *Regulation*.

In order to maintain its independence, the Cato Institute accepts no government funding. Contributions are received from foundations, corporations, and individuals, and other revenue is generated from the sale of publications. The Institute is a nonprofit, tax-exempt, educational foundation under Section 501(c)3 of the Internal Revenue Code.

CATO INSTITUTE
1000 Massachusetts Ave., N.W.
Washington, D.C. 20001